Diana
PRINCESS OF WALES

Diana
PRINCESS OF WALES

Nicholas Courtney

FOR VANESSA

First published in 1982 by Park Lane Press,
40 Park Street, London W1Y 4DE

Text copyright: © Nicholas Courtney 1982

Editor: Fiona Roxburgh
Designer: Martin Bristow

Text set by SX Composing Ltd, Rayleigh, Essex
Printed and bound by Henri Proost & Cie PVBA, Turnhout, Belgium

HALF TITLE: Lady Diana on her first visit to Tetbury in May 1981
FRONTISPIECE: The Princess of Wales on her wedding day photographed
by Lord Lichfield in the Throne Room at Buckingham Palace

Acknowledgments

The publishers would like to thank the following for permission to reproduce
illustrations: Reproduced by Gracious Permission of Her Majesty the Queen: 77
(*below*) and 78; Associated Newspapers: 18; Theo Bergström: 55 (*above*); Camera
Press Ltd (Photo Lichfield): *frontispiece*, 38, 46 (*both*) and 47 (*above*); (Photo Snowdon):
33; Central Press Photos Ltd: 8, 9, 36 (*above*), 67 and 69 (*above*); Tim Graham: *front and
back cover*, 7 (*both*), 17, 21, 23, 27, 28, 30, 32, 35 (*below*), 36 (*below left*), 37 (*both*), 48, 49,
(*above*), 50 (*below*), 53, 58, 59 (*both*), 60 (*above right*), 63 (*below left and right*), 64, 66, 68,
69 (*below*), 70 (*both*), 72 (*above*), 73 (*both*), 74 and 75; Peter A. Harding, Tetbury: 72
(*below*); Anwar Hussein: 20, 24, 29 (*below*), 31, 34 (*above*), 42, 49 (*below*), 50 (*above*), 54
(*both*), 56, 57, 60 (*below*), 62 and 65; London Express and News Features Services: 22;
Lynn News and Advertiser: 10 (*below*); Magdalen College, Oxford (Photo Weiden-
feld and Nicolson): 76; Mary Evans Picture Library: 77 (*above*) and 79 (*above*);
National Portrait Gallery: 79 (*below*) and 80; Norfolk Fire Service (Photo R. Good-
child): 16; Photographers International: 51; The Press Association Ltd: 6, 10 (*above*),
11, 12, 39, 40, 43 and 47 (*below*); Sir Geoffrey Shakerley: 19; The Rt. Hon. Earl
Spencer MVO, Althorp: 14 and 15; Frank Spooner Ltd (Gamma, Paris): 25, 26, 55
(*below*) and 71; Syndication International: *half-title*, 13, 29 (*above*), 34 (*below*), 36
(*below* right), 41, 44, 45, 52, 60 (*above left*) and 61; Gert Treuhaft: 63 (*above*); Wedgwood; 35 (*above*).

 Contents

Chapter One   CHILDHOOD 6

Chapter Two   LONDON LIFE 18

Chapter Three   COURTSHIP 24

Chapter Four   ENGAGEMENT 33

Chapter Five   WEDDING DAY 39

Chapter Six   HONEYMOON 48

Chapter Seven   BALMORAL HOLIDAY 53

Chapter Eight   TOUR OF WALES 57

Chapter Nine   HOMES AND PALACES 62

Chapter Ten   MARRIED LIFE 65

Chapter Eleven   PRINCESSES OF WALES 76

Childhood

Diana, aged seven, photographed with her brother Charles in 1968

You can just make out the tall chimneys and pointed gables of Park House from an attic window of Sandringham – the much loved home of the Royal Family for over a hundred years. A path, quite narrow, leads from the end of the west terrace, skirts round tidy, sweeping lawns, winds through ornamental trees and flowering shrubs beside the lake, on and up towards the parish church and the cricket field not far beyond. There, behind the boundary fence, lies Park House with its Lebanon cedar and ample gardens. Not a particularly inspiring house, it was built of a soft peaty stone towards the end of Queen Victoria's reign for the Prince of Wales's comptroller and since then it

has been kept for equerries or friends of the Royal Family. The house stands empty now, too large for modern living. But it is nonetheless an important house, for it is the birthplace of our Princess of Wales.

Late on the warm, sunny afternoon of Saturday, 1 July 1961 the Honourable Diana Spencer was born in her parents' bedroom in Park House. It was the very same room that her mother, Viscountess Althorp had been born in twenty-five years before. Her father was Edward John Spencer, Viscount Althorp and heir to the 7th Earl Spencer.

The confinement, through those last sweltering days of June, had been trouble free and the birth an 'easy delivery'. According to her father the baby, who weighed 7lb 12oz, was 'a superb physical specimen'. There must have been considerable relief and pleasure at so healthy a baby, for their son, John, born just the year before, lived only one day.

The proud parents had married in Westminster Abbey in June 1954, a glittering wedding officiated by a family friend, the Right Reverend Percy Herbert, Bishop of Norwich. Although retired as bishop, he returned to the little Sandringham church to christen their baby, Diana Frances, Diana after two Spencer ancestresses and Frances after her mother. One of her godmothers was the Lady Mary Colman, a Bowes-Lyon niece of the Queen Mother. Their two other children, Sarah and Jane had been christened in the same church, six and four years before, as was Charles, the long-awaited son and heir, three years later.

Diana's roots are firmly in Norfolk. Her maternal grandfather, Maurice and his identical twin Francis, had been brought up and educated in America and moved to Norfolk when he, the elder by twenty minutes, succeeded to the title of Fermoy as the 4th Baron in 1920. An avid politician, he finally became the Unionist (Conservative) member of Parliament for King's Lynn – a seat that he was to hold from 1924 to 1935 and again for the last two years of World War II. When he was forty-six, he met in Paris a young pupil of the pianist Alfred Cortot who was studying at the *Conservatoire*. She was Ruth Sylvia Gill, the daughter of another twin, William Gill of Aberdeenshire. They married in 1931 – the year in which the respected Lord Fermoy was elected Mayor of King's Lynn. The Fermoys had long been friends of King George V and Queen Mary, and when the lease of Park House became vacant the King granted it to them. They were not neighbours for long, for the King died in January 1936 – the very day on which the Fermoys' second daughter, Frances Ruth Burke Roche, was born. There is a family story that Queen Mary was able to tell the King the news just before he died.

This close association with the Royal Family was to develop even further, for King George VI and Queen Elizabeth had much in common with the Fermoys. They shared a love of country life, especially Norfolk, of shooting and tennis; both the King and Lord Fermoy being excellent shots and a good match for each other on court.

Besides Frances and her elder sister Cynthia, the Fermoys had one son, Edmund, born in 1939. Life in the nursery at Park House was little different to the one enjoyed in the next generation. Holidays were always active, spent mostly outdoors with their friends – the children of the neighbouring estates – or pottering around the Sandringham Estate. The house was always full of their cousins or their parents' friends. School was

TOP: *Park House, Diana's birthplace and childhood home*
ABOVE: *Sandringham House, the Norfolk home of the Royal Family*

slightly more serious. Lessons were held in the schoolroom with a few of their neighbours' children under the supervision of a governess, Miss Gertrude Allen, affectionately known as 'Gert'. When old enough, the girls both went to Downham in Hertfordshire, a particularly smart boarding school specialising in the daughters of the Norfolk aristocracy. Frances did particularly well, leaving at the age of sixteen as head girl and captain of lacrosse, netball, cricket and of course tennis with her father's coaching.

During that summer of 1952, Frances met the Viscount Althorp,

Johnny as he was affectionately known to his family and freiends. At that time, he was Equerry to the young Queen Elizabeth, a valued court position gained through experience. For two years this handsome captain in the Scots Greys, a fine Scottish cavalry regiment, had been Equerry to the late King George VI and before that ADC to the Governor-General of South Australia. Johnny was 'the catch' of the county, for the Spencers are one of the great families of England with large estates and a beautiful house in Northamptonshire, Althorp (pronounced Alltrup) filled with

Viscount Althorp (in the centre) was acting Master of the Queen's Household during the Queen and Prince Philip's first Commonwealth tour of Australia and New Zealand in 1954. For the investiture, the Queen wore a diamond tiara which had formerly belonged to her grandmother, Queen Mary, and which many years later was to be the Queen's wedding present to her daughter-in-law and Viscount Althorp's youngest daughter.

a member of the Queen's household they remained great friends – his name appears regularly in Prince Philip's game book as one of the guns at a Sandringham or Balmoral shoot. Their's was a busy life with Frances supervising the running of her house, the nursery (Sarah was born in 1955 and Jane two years later), the dogs, a few favourite charities and much entertaining, while he farmed not far away.

In 1961, Diana came as a happy addition to that contented family. She was an even-tempered baby, adored by her parents and looked after by a young nanny from Kent, Judith Parnell. Her father, with a transparent note of affection, was to describe her later as 'a delightful child, and as a baby she could have won any beauty competition'. Although she grew up in this rarefied atmosphere of privilege and love neither she, nor her sisters, were spoilt. Being the youngest of three girls, Diana commanded the most attention of her mother – at least for the first three years of her life. Then, the long-awaited son and heir, Charles, arrived and Diana's 'baby days' were over.

She joined her sisters in the schoolroom under her mother's old governess, Miss Gertrude Allen. The only difference between Diana's early schooling and her mother's was that Miss Allen was called 'Ally' to this generation and the schoolroom had been moved from a room beside the front door to the butler's pantry.

'Ally' had spent her life in Norfolk as a governess, and taught with a mixture of firmness and humour. In the schoolroom, with its leaves and balloon wallpaper, Diana was taught the four 'Rs', reading, 'riting and 'rithmatic (the fourth R stands for riding). 'Ally' remembers her as a 'relaxed child but somewhat serious' and 'a tidy soul'. She was described as a 'conscientious worker' and a 'real trier'. Like all children she loved stories and was fond of history – kings and queens, 'not battles'. Such an interest would be only natural in a girl whose neighbours, whom she saw at odd intervals throughout the year, were queens, princesses and princes – in particular Prince Andrew, her contemporary, and Prince Edward, his younger brother.

As Diana grew up, she discovered the same pleasures of the countryside that her mother had found as a child. She took the same walks, built houses

magnificent furniture and one of the finest private collection of pictures in Britain.

By the time Lord Althorp left for Australia as Master of the Household on the Queen and Prince Philip's first Commonwealth tour of Australia and New Zealand, he and Frances Roche were unofficially engaged. They wrote to each other daily during that six-month tour and when the Royal Party teached Tobruk on the way home, he was allowed to return to London to prepare for his wedding.

At eighteen, Frances was the youngest bride to be married in Westminster Abbey this century. The

Queen, Prince Philip, the Queen Mother and Princess Margaret were among the 1,500 guests who witnessed the splendid ceremony.

The Althorps began their married life in Gloucestershire where he attended the Estate Management course at the Royal Agricultural College, Cirencester. After the first year, Frances's father died and as Park House was too large for Lady Fermoy, the Althorps took over the lease and moved back to her old home.

Those early years of their marriage were particularly happy. They were established pillars of Norfolk society and although Althorp was no longer

in the same trees and went to the same homes for children's parties, even playing the same games as her mother had done. Holidays were always spent in Norfolk, or with cousins, for there was little point in substituting their own piece of Norfolk coastline for another elsewhere in the country. The Spencer children spent much of their time in the stables where they kept their animals; Sarah's scruffy pony, Jane's rabbits 'and anything small enough to go in a cage' like hamsters, gerbels or guinea pigs were for Diana. Their parents' dogs, mostly springer spaniels, also played a major part of their nursery life. Sarah, being the eldest, was by far the most extrovert and naturally became the leader. Jane was quieter and happy to be led by her more forceful sister. Somewhere between the two in temperament came Diana, who was growing up as a thoughtful child – she was always the

Viscount Althorp and his bride, Diana's parents, leaving Westminster Abbey after their marriage on 1 June 1954

first to put another log on the fire and the first to close the shutters at night.

Then, when Diana was six, came the biggest upset to that enchanted childhood – her mother and father separated and, after a bitter series of court actions, were divorced in 1969. In retrospect, it may be that this terrible shock and the storm of publicity that followed, gave Diana the steel and fortitude years later to cope with the trials of her new life as the Princess of Wales.

Life at Park House continued without Lady Althorp – she had gone off with Peter Shand Kydd, whom she married two years later. A series of *au pairs* were engaged but none stayed for long. Althorp coped as best he

could with his house and children but their real saviour was Ruth, Lady Fermoy. She stepped in with tact and advice, partially filling the void left by their mother.

Lady Fermoy gave them all the time she could spare, and more. She is an active woman, who like so many of Diana's family, holds a position at court as Lady in Waiting to the Queen Elizabeth, the Queen Mother. At that time she was a Woman of the Bedchamber, a position she relinquished in 1981 after nearly twenty-five years service. She also founded and ran the highly acclaimed King's Lynn Festival of Music and Arts.

When Diana was seven she had outgrown the schoolroom and 'Ally'. She followed her sisters to a day school, Silfield, in King's Lynn. There was a regular school run from the Sandringham Estate shared with Alexandra Loyd, the daughter of Julian Loyd,

ABOVE: *Diana on her first birthday on the lawn at Park House*
RIGHT: *Diana, aged nearly three, at her uncle Lord Fermoy's wedding*

the Queen's land agent. Alexandra, like all Diana's childhood friends, is as close now as then. As a special prize for trying hard, Diana's father imported a camel, called Bert, from Dudley Zoo for her seventh birthday party. Diana's next birthday was also memorable for it fell on the same day as the Investiture of the Prince of Wales at Caernarvon Castle on 1 July 1969. It was also during these holidays that she fell off a pony and broke her arm. It took over two months to mend and she completely lost her nerve for riding horses.

The family rift was partially healed when Diana's mother married Peter Shand Kydd in 1969. Part of each school holidays was now spent with her mother and step-father at their house in Itchenor, in West Sussex, or at her mother's flat in Cadogan Place, sometimes with Peter Shand Kydd's three children by his former marriage.

When she reached the age of nine, it was decided that Diana was old enough to go away to school. Her father remembers it as 'a dreadful day, dreadful losing her'. Dressed in her school uniform from Harrods of cherry sweater, white shirt and a grey pleated skirt she arrived at Riddles-

worth Hall, near Diss in Norfolk, for the Michaelmas term in 1970. Her trunk was marked a plain 'D. Spencer' and her tuck box was filled with her favourite treats – chocolate cakes, ginger biscuits and Twiglets. Riddlesworth was an ideal choice with its its country-house atmosphere and understanding headmistress, Miss Elizabeth Ridsdale. 'Riddy' as she was known, had been headmistress for over twenty years and in that time had had much experience with girls from broken homes. Riddlesworth also suited Diana as she had many of her Norfolk friends with her, it was only forty miles from her home and she was allowed to keep her guinea pigs, including the tan and white prize winner called Peanuts, in hutches in the grounds.

Diana was to stay there for three years. Her contemporaries remember her as a particularly spirited girl, the younger ones rather in awe of her for the pranks she played so successfully. Miss Ridsdale remembers her as 'a decent kind little girl. Everyone seemed to like her . . . She was good at games, especially swimming, which was very well taught at the school. She took part in everything . . . What stands out in my mind is how awfully

RIGHT: *Diana on holiday with her mother at Itchenor on the Sussex coast during the summer of 1970*

sweet she was with the little ones.'

As Downham, her mother's school had closed down, Diana sat her Common Entrance exam for West Heath, a girls public school near Sevenoaks and passed 'quite well'. Part of that summer holiday was spent at Park House with its new attraction of a heated outdoor swimming pool and tennis, with the local tournaments and coaching from a Mrs Lansdowne. The rest of the time was spent in Scotland with her mother, who was now living on their 1,000-acre hill farm on the Isle of Seil, near Oban in Argyllshire. It was the first of many happy holidays to be spent in Scotland. The horror of the separation and the divorce long over, mother and daughter grew especially close. Part of that strong, forceful character of the new Mrs Shand Kydd was to rub off onto Diana. Even as a child of twelve, she became self reliant and thoroughly domesticated. The Shand Kydd's life at Ardencaple, their whitewashed farm house, was healthy, fun and active. When not helping on the farm, Diana and any of her friends and family who were staying, would explore the small island, 'the Bridge over the Atlantic' built by Telford in 1792 or the heather

Diana visited her mother in Argyllshire during the school holidays. She is seen here in 1974 with her mother's Shetland pony, Soufflé.

hills on the mainland. There was always plenty to do, the lobster pots to be baited, put down and collected, trolling for mackerel, sailing in her step-father's boat – even swimming, although she was the only one to brave the cold Atlantic waters.

West Heath was another good choice of schools for Diana. She arrived for the Michaelmas term of 1973 with a Norfolk friend, Carolyn Harbord Hammond, who had also been at Riddlesworth with her. The headmistress, Miss Ruth Rudge, believed in fostering the individuality of each of her 130 pupils and ran the school with a blend of firmness and kindness. She encouraged her pupils 'to develop their own minds and tastes and to realize their own duties as citizens'.

Diana's academic record was unremarkable. Her reports were peppered with 'average' or 'normal' although 'tried hard' was more usual. Her prowess lay in other areas – most noticeably on the sports field. She was to become captain of hockey but

where she excelled, was at swimming. She carried off all the cups for the school and other inter-school trophies. Music was another 'taste' that was well catered for at West Heath. Diana started learning the piano but abandoned her lessons in favour of ballet and tap dancing. She had had lessons since she was three and a half and wanted to become a ballet dancer but she grew too tall.

It was her 'duty as a citizen', that West Heath criterion, that gave Diana the most pleasure. Every week she visited an old woman, talking to her, doing the odd job about the house, also shopping for her. Another afternoon a week she used to visit a centre for handicapped children. She would play with the children, read to them or help the staff with any chore. It was this willingness to help and cheerful personality that earned Diana 'a special award for service'. It was a discretionary award, only presented to outstanding pupils and Miss Rudge believed that 'Diana was genuinely surprised to have won it'.

Just before her fourteenth birthday, Diana's paternal grandfather died and her father succeeded him as the 8th Earl Spencer. Diana, who was now the daughter of an earl, became The

Lady Diana Spencer. The other change was that the family left Park House to move to the Spencer family seat, Althorp in Northamptonshire. Despite its enormous size and fabulous treasures, Althorp is a family home. Her father remembers her, in those early days, 'flying down the front staircase on a tea-tray' or playing 'bears in the park' amongst the rows of her forebears in the long picture gallery. Later, she and her brother Charles, were to be seen in a bright blue beach buggy driving round the estate. A heated open-air swimming pool was installed almost immediately.

Soon after their move to Althorp, there was a dramatic event that was to affect the whole family. Earl Spencer had known the Earl of Dartmouth practically all his life – they had been in the same house at Eton – and consequently knew his wife, the Countess of Darmouth. She was Raine, the daughter of the romantic novelist Barbara Cartland and somewhat of a public figure in her own right. She made frequent television appearances and had been elected as a Westminster City councillor, later sitting on the Greater London Council. A forceful woman, she campaigned vigorously for cleanliness causes – both moral and physical. This friendship grew between Earl Spencer and the Countess

of Dartmouth to the point where she left her husband and moved into Althorp. No secret was made of the fact that she was resented by his children and the staff by her mere presence and her sweeping changes to the house and estate. Two years later, Dartmouth was granted a divorce on the grounds that his marriage had broken down and she now was free to marry Lord Spencer. None of the children attended the wedding in a London registry office. This was seen as a snub but in fact none of the children was told until after the ceremony had taken place. For the second time in her short life, Lady Diana was to experience exposure of her family in the press and to learn to cope with it.

Whatever the children thought of their 'wicked step-mother', they do at least have her to thank for their father's life. On 9 September 1978, shortly after a ball given at Althorp to celebrate the final settlement of his father's estate duty, Earl Spencer collapsed in the stable block with a massive brain haemorrhage. For four months Countess Spencer nursed her husband, moving him from hospital to hospital in search of the best medical treatment. She used her influence to

The main building of West Heath School near Sevenoaks in Kent

obtain a new and untested drug from Germany. The drug and her constant effort worked and he is now fully recovered, save for a slight impediment in his speech.

Towards the end of Lady Diana's last term at West Heath, Miss Rudge allowed her home to Althorp for a special weekend – Prince Charles, a friend of her sister Sarah, had been invited to shoot. Lady Diana was driven up from Kent early on the Saturday morning and joined the guns on the last drive before lunch. On that glorious November morning, in the middle of a ploughed field, the Prince of Wales first met his future bride.

The Spencers have been inextricably linked by service and blood ties with the sovereign since before the Norman Conquest. Lady Diana and the Prince of Wales are related several times over – they are eleventh cousins once removed from James I, or sixteenth cousins once removed with a common ancestor in Henry VII. Closer to hand, they are seventh cousins once removed through William Cavendish, the 3rd Duke of Devonshire. The more direct links between the two families are through the illegitimate progeny of Charles II, and an illegitimate daughter of James II and Arabella Churchill, who was the daughter of the first Sir Winston

Churchill, and sister of the first Duke of Marlborough.

Although prominent as a family in the fifteenth century, the Spencer fortunes were firmly established in 1506, when Sir John Spencer bought the two Manors of Wormleighton in Warwickshire and Althorp with its moated, red brick house in Northamptonshire. The finance for such a venture had come from extensive sheep farming and wool trading. His grandson, another Sir John and former Lord Mayor of London, added the wings to the house although he continued to live in Warwickshire. The first Lord Spencer was Sir John's grandson, formerly Sir Robert Spencer, and was reputedly the richest man in England with his sheep, cattle and cereal dealings.

The third Lord Spencer, a devoted follower of Charles I, was created Earl of Sunderland in recognition of his loan to the King of £10,000. He was killed four months later at the first Battle of Newbury in 1643. The second Earl of Sunderland, Robert, was a ruthless character. A brilliant,

Althorp in 1677 painted by Sir John Vorsterman. Most of the fine earlier paintings and furniture at Althorp today were collected in the seventeenth century by the gifted Robert Spencer, 2nd Earl of Sunderland.

but devious politician he made himself indispensible as chief adviser to three monarchs, Charles II, James II and William III by switching religion and loyalties to his best advantage. Most of the fine, earlier paintings and furniture at Althorp today were collected by him. He commissioned an Italian architect to remodel the house and imported Le Nôtre, the designer of the gardens at Versailles, to lay out the elm avenue.

The third Earl was another politician and a prominent member of the court of Queen Anne and later George I. Despite his rash temper and the intrigues of his rivals he became, like his father, the Lord President of the Council and later First Lord of the Treasury. Before he died, of suspected poisoning in 1722, he collected an outstanding library. He married three

times, his second wife being Lady Anne Churchill, the co-heiress to the great Duke of Marlborough as the famous commander had no surviving son. They had five children together, three of them sons. The first became the fourth Earl of Sunderland who in turn was succeeded by his brother, Charles as the fifth Earl. He then succeeded, by special letters patent, as the 3rd Duke of Marlborough and thus inherited Blenheim Palace in Oxfordshire.

The youngest son, the Honourable John Spencer, known as Jack, not only inherited Althorp and its considerable riches but also vast tracts of land and treasures from his doting grandmother, Sarah, Duchess of Marlborough. His youngest sister, the Lady Diana, was close to becoming the Princess of Wales. The scheming old Duchess of Marlborough offered a dowry of £100,000 if Frederick

RIGHT: *Lady Henrietta Spencer, one of the famous Spencer sisters renowned for their wit and dazzling beauty in the mid-eighteenth century*

Louis, Prince of Wales and son of George II, would marry her favourite granddaughter. The Prince, deep in debt, readily accepted and the wedding was due to take place at the Duchess's house in Windsor Great Park. The Duchess of Marlborough had not bargained for the spies of the Prime Minister, Sir Robert Walpole, who rumbled the plan and the match was stopped. Lady Diana later married the Duke of Bedford.

Jack Spencer died when he was only thirty-eight in 1746, 'merely because he would not be abridged of those invaluable blessings of an English subject – brandy, small beer and tobacco' was the reason given by Horace Walpole. Jack Spencer's son, another John Spencer was created the first Earl Spencer in 1765. He is remembered not only as a patron of the arts, who added the works of Reynolds, Gainsborough and Stubbs to the Althorp collection but also as the father of two of the most remarkable women of the age – the Lady Georgiana and the Lady Henrietta Spencer. They dazzled London society with their wit, beauty, morals and charm. Georgiana, 'the face without a frown', married the Duke of Devonshire when aged seventeen while her sister became the Countess of Bessborough.

Their brother, George John, became the second Earl in 1783. He had a distinguished career as Ambassador to Vienna, Lord Privy Seal, then First Lord of the Admiralty and ending up as Secretary of State. His real passion was books and he collected the finest library in Europe, a collection that included fifty-eight books printed by Caxton.

The third Earl, John Charles, after an unprepossessing start as a boy ended as the Leader of the House of Commons and later as the Chancellor of the Exchequer. A great farming innovator, he founded the Royal Agricultural Society of England as well as the Royal Agricultural College, Cirencester. He was succeeded by his brother, Frederick who had distinguished himself in the Royal Navy, in Parliament and later at court as a Privy Councillor and Lord Chamberlain.

He, in turn, was succeeded by his only son, John Poyntz the fifth Earl, known as the Red Earl on account of his bushy beard. In true Spencer fashion he was a loyal courtier, being Groom to the Stole to Prince Albert

and to the Prince of Wales, later Edward VII. The King was to be served by another Earl Spencer, Charles Robert, the Red Earl's half brother. He succeeded as the sixth Earl in 1910 but he had been created Viscount Althorp on his appointment as Lord Chamberlain in 1905.

His son, the present Earl Spencer's father, was Albert John, the seventh Earl. Known as 'Jack' he devoted himself to the conservation of Althorp, but also served on outside fine art bodies. That generation of Spencers had a fine record of service to the Queen Mother for his wife, Lady Cynthia, daughter of the Duke of Abercorn and his sisters, Lady Delia, married to Sir Sydney Peel and Lady Lavinia, married to Lord Annaly, were all Women of the Bedchamber. Following in their footsteps, the present Earl Spencer has been Equerry

to King George VI and to the Queen. He is chairman of the National Association of Boys Clubs and works for many other charitable bodies. He is proud to live at 'Althorp, with its breathtaking collection of treasures, which remains as a testimonial to all those Spencers who not only gave their time and energies in public service, but managed to add their own special contribution to the house.'

Lady Diana's ancestors on her mother's side are no less noble, although they cannot boast descent from a sovereign. The Fermoys, whose family name is Roche, are descended from Adam de Rupe of Roch Castle, Pembrokeshire, who invaded Ireland with 'Strongbow' in the reign of Henry II. David Roche was created Lord Fermoy by Edward IV. During the Civil War, their lands in Ireland were confiscated by Oliver

The 4th Baron Fermoy, Diana's grandfather, photographed in 1930

Cromwell and they failed to regain them after the Restoration in 1660. That branch of the family and the title died out in 1733.

The present Roche family is descended from a kinsman, Maurice FitzEdmund Roche of Trabolgan, near Whitegate on the south coast of County Cork. Unlike Lord Fermoy, the Trabolgan Roches managed to keep their estate despite their allegiance to Charles I.

The present Barony of Fermoy dates from 1856 when Queen Victoria conferred it on Edmund Burke Roche. He had been Member of Parliament and Lord Lieutenant for County Cork. The family name of Burke came through his mother, Margaret Honoria Curtain, a close relation of that great Whig statesman,

Althorp, the handsome Northampton-shire Spencer family home

Edmund Burke. The title passed first to his eldest son, Edward, who died childless, then to his second son James; the youngest son, Alexis, was a gentleman in waiting to the viceregal court of Ireland.

James Boothby Burke, 3rd Baron Fermoy, married an American heiress, Frances Work, the daughter of a New York banker. It is through this American connection that the Princess of Wales is seventh cousin to both Humphrey Bogart and Rudolf Valentino. Lord Fermoy divorced his wife in 1891 and his twin sons were brought up as Americans by their maternal grandfather and also benefited from his considerable will. The

elder twin, Maurice, the Princess of Wales's grandfather, succeeded his father in 1920 at the age of thirty-five. Like so many of her family on both sides, he too was a politician, a close friend of three generations of the Royal Family and married to a Woman of the Bedchamber.

When the Queen was told of the engagement of the Prince of Wales to the Lady Diana Spencer, she can have had no qualms as to her suitability. She had known this nineteen-year-old girl since birth, her beauty, charm and love of her son and capacity to make him happy were self-evident but, almost as a bonus, her breeding was impeccable and the service and loyalty to the throne of both sides of her family had been constant for countless generations.

CHAPTER TWO

London Life

Lady Diana enjoying a dance during her term at the Institut Alpin Videmanette near Gstaad in Switzerland

There is no exact point in a girl's life when you can say that she is a child or that she is an adult. For Lady Diana, whose upbringing to some could be termed as old-fashioned, the November weekend that the Prince of Wales came to shoot was a turning point in her life. Her father, much impressed with her, her immaculate appearance and the way she conducted herself at dinner that night, was very proud of his youngest daughter.

Against her father's advice, but with both her parents' blessing, Lady Diana left West Heath at the end of that term. Her mother suggested that she went to the same finishing school in Switzerland that her sister Sarah had enjoyed six years earlier. The

following January, 1978, Lady Diana went to the Institut Alpin Videmanette at the Château d'Oex near Gstaad. In that single term she took lessons in French and Swiss cooking, and dressmaking with a little typing. What was to be more useful to her, she improved her French and spent every afternoon skiing in what was the smartest resort in Switzerland. The headmistress, Madame Yersin, used to the more sophisticated Continental girls, said of her latest English pupil, 'When Diana arrived she was a lovely girl – but rather young

for a sixteen-year-old and while she was a pretty girl, she was not the beauty she's blossomed into now'. Occasionally they were allowed to the village of Gstaad, heavily chaperoned, to some of the night clubs. The sixty girls at the Institut were encouraged to work and play hard in that family atmosphere, but Lady Diana felt that it was too much like an extension of her boarding school life. Her French mistress commented later that they '. . . discussed life in general and what the girls wanted to do. Lady Diana was broad-minded, but she was also very idealistic. She knew she wanted to work with children – and then she wanted to get married and have children of her own.' Little did she

know then those three ambitions would be fulfilled within five years.

There was much excited chatter at the Institut when the Prince of Wales arrived at nearby Klosters with Lady Sarah for their skiing holiday. Their presence must have affected Lady Diana for her headmistress was to remark, possibly with hindsight, 'We've heard that she was secretly in love with Prince Charles. If so, the publicity about Lady Sarah must have been hard on her. Things like that are very difficult for a girl of that age to cope with.'

The press were to report much later that Lady Diana left Château d'Oex because she was home-sick, but that was totally out of character.

Lady Diana was chief bridesmaid to her sister, Lady Jane, when she married Robert Fellowes in April 1978. The reception was held at St James's Palace.

The real reason was simpler, she 'did not want to spend the summer just picking Alpine flowers'. Another reason was that she did not wish to miss the excitement of her middle sister Jane's twenty-first birthday party and the preparations for her wedding where Diana was to be the chief bridesmaid. Lady Jane married Robert Fellowes, the Queen's assistant private secretary and son of her former land agent at Sandringham, Sir Billy Fellowes and of course a

neighbour of the Spencers when they lived at Park House.

As Mrs Shand Kydd was firmly esconced in Scotland or in Australia (she had bought a sheep 'station' near Young in New South Wales next to her husband Peter's station called Yass), her flat in Cadogan Place in London was unoccupied for most of the year. Lady Diana moved in towards the end of March with a girl-friend, Sophie Kimball, the daughter of Gainsborough's Conservative MP, Marcus Kimball, with a third member of the flat changing fairly regularly.

It was typical of Lady Diana not to conform to the life usually led by a girl with her background who has just come to London. Not for her the 'deb' season with its endless cocktail parties and social chatter, charity dances and frivolous tea parties or nights spent in expensive restaurants and *chi chi* night clubs. Instead, she set about fulfilling the first of her three ambitions – looking after children. She became an unpaid nanny to various of her married friends, helping out wherever she was most needed. There is one little boy, an American named Patrick, who will never forget her, with good reason. Lady Diana, plain Diana to him, spent two afternoons a week for well over a year, reading, telling stories or inventing games for him to play.

To Lady Diana, her London life was an extension of her life in the country in Norfolk, Northamptonshire and Scotland. She kept her childhood and school friends, later adding their brothers and their friends to her circle.

She gave small dinner parties in her flat where the food was even more delicious after her Cordon Bleu cookery course with Elizabeth Russell in Wimbledon. Although there was always plenty for her guests to drink, Lady Diana never touches alcohol, neither does she smoke. Her dinners were amusing too, for Lady Diana is renowned as a mimic and impersonator, Miss Piggy from the Muppets being her *tour de force*. Conversation would range from general gossip of friends and happenings to the cinema, theatre and opera. Lady Diana has always been particularly interested in the arts. Other guests, like Harry Herbert, the Earl of Caernarvon's grandson, and Simon Berry, were accomplished amateur actors. Their production of William Douglas-Home's *The Reluctant Debutant* in 1980 raised over £4,500 for the Cancer Relief Fund.

Another landmark in Lady Diana's life was her London flat in Coleherne Court, a joint gift from her parents in July 1979. This first-floor flat had three bedrooms, a pretty sitting room overlooking the Old Brompton Road and the fashionable Little Boltons. True to form, Lady Diana roped in many of her friends and painted it herself – the sitting room in pale primrose yellow, a foil for the yellow floral chintz curtains and oatmeal-coloured sofa, and her bedroom in a soft green. The hall, with its tangle of bicycles, had an open trellis wallpaper while the bathroom and loo were papered in bright red cherries. A circular table in the large kitchen served as the dining room. A friend from West Heath, Carolyn Pride, was the first of three flatmates; Anne Bolton and Virginia Pitman came a little later.

Theirs was an exceptionally happy flat where everything was discussed between them. Lady Diana loves shopping, particularly for clothes, and takes great care in choosing her wardrobe. She bought from a variety of shops, from Fiorucci for her jeans – which suited her well with her long legs – to her suits and evening dresses which came from Harrods and later from Emanuel. She has that knack of wearing clothes well, so that she did not need to spend a fortune in order to look smart. Thus, a modest article from Laura Ashley or Benetton on her looked chic and expensive. Her jewellery was modest, a few gifts from her mother, a string of pearls, all always worn to the best effect.

By the time Lady Diana had moved into her new flat, she had already started to help out at a kindergarten school in a Pimlico church hall. She was recruited by one of their mistresses, a West Heath school friend, Kay Seth-Smith. Mrs Victoria Wilson, who started and ran The Young England Kindergarten School, catered for about fifty 'under-fives' – the children of the better-off local residents. There, her true talent with children came to the fore. She was an instant success, despite having no formal training with children. Her mother described her as 'a positive pied-piper with children'. Lady Diana had that rare gift of treating each child as if he or she were the only one that mattered and in turn they all adored her, remembering 'Miss Diana' particularly for her kindness and her involuntary giggle.

Weekends were usually spent in the country, either at Althorp – with her father or with her sister Jane who had a farmhouse on the estate – or at a friend's house party. Lady Diana visited her mother as often as she could. She would spend the summer months in Scotland, staying with her mother on the Isle of Seil or with a friend like Caroline Harbord Hammond, whose parents have a cottage on the neighbouring Isle of Mull, or Sophie Kimball at her parents' house at Lairg in the Highlands. Her biggest invitation, in August 1979, was to stay at Balmoral as a guest of the Queen and Prince Philip, to join the 'younger group' headed by Prince Andrew. Of course, she had known her hosts and the Prince all her life from those early days at Sandringham and more recently, from two previous visits to Balmoral. Although the Prince of Wales was there, he had his own friends staying and spent most of his time with them either fishing or shooting. He simply took a friendly interest in this pretty, eighteen-year-old companion of his younger

Coleherne Court in the Old Brompton Road where Lady Diana lived in London until the day her engagement was announced

RIGHT: *Lady Diana outside The Young England Kindergarten School in Pimlico*

Prince Charles windsurfing during his visit to the Cowes Week regatta in 1980

brother. Lady Diana and Prince Andrew certainly made a handsome couple but there was never a hint of a romance.

It is always exciting to return to the place of your childhood – so it was doubly thrilling for Lady Diana, in February 1980, to be asked to stay at Wood Farm, the farm house on the Sandringham estate the Royal Family use when not staying at 'The Big House'. She travelled up that familiar line to King's Lynn station with Amanda Knatchbull, the grand-daughter of the late Earl Mountbatten. Again, the Prince of Wales was pleased to see her but was more occupied with his own friends.

'Miss' Diana continued to teach at Young England, completely un-affected by her Royal associations and invitations. The next invitation, however, was to have the greatest affect on her life. The Prince of Wales asked Lady Diana to join his party one Sunday in July at Cowdray Park in Sussex where the polo team he plays for, Les Diables Bleus, was competing

LEFT: *Lady Diana outside Coleherne Court before the engagement was announced*

in the Gold Cup tournament. A few weeks later, Lady Diana was staying on the Royal Yacht *Britannia* moored in Cowes Roads for the famous yachting regatta, Cowes Week. Prince Philip invited her to join what was a young party with Prince Andrew, Prince Edward and their cousins, James and Marina Ogilvy and, of course, the Prince of Wales. In one of Lady Diana's frequent moments of fun, she flipped the mast of Prince Charles's windsurfer, duck-ing him into the Solent.

The rest of that summer was spent in Scotland and Lady Diana returned to Balmoral, ostensibly to be with Robert and Jane Fellowes and their new-born baby. During that time, in the relaxed atmosphere of the Castle and the mountains, rivers and glens of the estate, Lady Diana and the Prince of Wales spent more and more of their time together. Then, just as they were sharing the enjoyment of each other's company, Lady Diana shared in his family tragedy. On August Bank Holiday Monday, Lady Diana was among the guests lunching

with the Queen when the news came of the brutal assassination of Earl Mountbatten, Prince Philip's favour-ite and much loved uncle. Being party to their private grief strengthened the bonds between her and the Prince of Wales and his family.

Over the next few days, the Prince of Wales took her often to watch him fishing on the Dee or on walks over the estate. She did not attend the Braemar Gathering with the rest of the Balmoral house party, nor 'kirk' on Sunday for fear of the 'posse' of photographers – ever since Prince Charles's break-up with his former girlfriend, Anna Wallace, the press had been thirsting for a replace-ment. One old hand knew where they might be. He was right and found the Prince of Wales fishing and saw the tip of a green wellington boot pro-truding from behind a tree and a hand mirror angled towards him, warning of his intrusion. The couple fled to another spot eight miles downstream but the photographer beat them to it and the next day, Monday 8 Septem-ber, their secret was out and an-nounced to the world. From then on, Lady Diana was headline news for the rest of her life.

23

CHAPTER THREE

Courtship

Lady Diana in September 1980 with two of her charges at The Young England Kindergarten in Pimlico

There can not have been a more bizarre courtship of any couple in the world, than that of the Prince of Wales and the Lady Diana Spencer. From the day that he was born, potential brides had been found for him by the world's press and any girl in his company was instantly dubbed by them 'a future queen'. Such interest in the world's most eligible bachelor was hardly surprising and when the new girl in his life was as young, beautiful and aristocratic as Lady Diana, the press went wild. For five months they were to dog her every move, speculate wildly and intrude into her life to such an extent that even questions were asked in both Houses of Parliament. The account of

their courtship is almost more a saga of the obtrusive behaviour of the press rather than of the couple's meetings.

Term started at the Young England Kindergarten soon after Lady Diana returned from Balmoral in September 1980. Her life continued on very much the same lines, save for the unwelcome attentions of the press. They followed her in droves from her flat to the school, one reporter even posed as a road sweeper to get closer, another was caught climbing in through the lavatory window. Photographers sat in the lecture room of the

local library opposite and spied with long lenses and binoculars into her bedroom and sitting-room windows. They telephoned at all hours of the day and night – to change the number would be to admit there was 'truth in the rumour'. Lady Diana coped with this unwarranted attention with ability far beyond her experience and slender years. Initially she believed that like her, the photographers had a job to do and she responded accordingly. She never allowed herself to be drawn nor caught with her guard down. Questions were parried with a

RIGHT: *Even when shopping Lady Diana was pursued by the press determined to link her name with Prince Charles*

smile or a blush. 'You know I can't say anything about the Prince or my feelings for him', she would reply when pressed. Other members of the Royal Family have a built-in system to protect them from such barrages but to have extended this to Lady Diana would have been taken as an official Buckingham Palace statement that their assertions were correct.

Part of this ordeal was born by her three flatmates, Carolyn Pride, Anne Bolton and Virginia Pitman. They devised a series of decoy manoeuvres in order to spirit Lady Diana out of her flat so she and the Prince of Wales could meet – whenever his busy schedule allowed. They were able to slip away together, unobserved, to stay for a few days in October with the Queen Mother at her home, Birkhall on the Balmoral estate. There, appropriately, Prince Charles gave Lady Diana an advance copy of his book, *The Old Man of Lochnagar*, a children's story set at Balmoral, originally written for his younger brothers.

Earl Mountbatten had prophesied that when Prince Charles found the girl he wanted to marry '. . . he will not ever be seen with her in public.

During the autumn of 1980, photographers literally camped day and night outside the London flat of Lady Diana in search of details of a possible royal romance.

Very privately he will try hard to win her round like any other suitor . . .' Earl Mountbatten was right and the Prince of Wales successfully kept their friendship secret and public interest began to wane.

That privacy did not last for long, for they were seen together on 24 October at Ludlow races in Shropshire. He was riding his horse Allibar in an amateur race, the Clun Handicap and his first ever race over fences. Lady Diana drove herself to the race meeting and backed him each way, luckily, as he finished second. They left separately, meeting at the Wiltshire home of Lieutenant-Colonel Andrew Parker Bowles and his wife, Camilla. Next morning, the men went cubbing with the Beaufort Hunt but when Lady Diana went to meet them in the drive, she had to retreat from the ever-attendant press.

They managed to slip away to Highgrove, near Tetbury in Gloucestershire and Prince Charles showed

off his home for the first time to Lady Diana. The press were waiting for them the next weekend when the Prince of Wales and Andrew Parker Bowles returned from the opening meet of the Beaufort Hunt but this time Lady Diana and Camilla stayed indoors.

Lady Diana's next 'public' appearance was on 4 November at the Ritz Hotel in London, at a ball given for Princess Margaret's fiftieth birthday by six of her closest friends. Now considered very much as 'family', she was included in the dinner for members of the Royal Family before the ball.

While it was intensely boring for Lady Diana being harried by newsmen, their articles, usually wildly inaccurate, were not generally offensive. That was until the *Sunday Mirror* printed a scurrilous piece stating that Lady Diana had spent the night with the Prince of Wales on the Royal Train in a siding outside Swindon. She had, in fact, gone to bed early in Coleherne Court being tired after Princess Margaret's dance the night before.

The Prince of Wales's thirty-second birthday fell on Friday, 14 November.

Rumours were rife that he would announce his engagement from Sandringham that day and Lady Diana was eagerly awaited by the rather cold throng of pressmen at the gate. However, Lady Diana was one step ahead of them as she 'escaped' from Coleherne Court, went by train to King's Lynn and then to Sandringham entering by a back entrance in an old Ford Cortina. The press had been fooled and their persistant presence provoked a 'haven't you got any wives to go to?' from an irate Prince Charles.

An official tour of the Prince of Wales to India and Nepal, then Christmas, separated them for nearly six weeks. While he was being photographed in his official capacity, Lady Diana was suffering in England. The episode of the Royal Train, dubbed 'Love in the Sidings' by Fleet Street, provoked an angry response from the Queen but the editor of the *Sunday Mirror* remained unrepentant. The incident prompted Mrs Shand Kydd to write from her home on the Isle of Seil to *The Times*.

In recent weeks many articles have been labelled 'exclusive quotes', when the plain truth is that my daughter has not spoken the words attributed to her. Fanciful speculation, if it is in good taste is one thing, but this can be embarrassing. Lies are quite another matter, and by their very nature, hurtful and inexcusable. May I ask the editors of Fleet Street whether, in the execution of their jobs, they consider it necessary or fair to harass my daughter daily, from dawn until well after dusk? Is it fair to ask any human being, regardless of circumstances, to be treated in this way? The freedom of the press was granted by law, by public demand, for very good reasons. But when these privileges are abused, can the press command any respect, or expect to be shown any respect?

The letter was a heartfelt cry from a mother for her vulnerable daughter. Sixty Members of Parliament took up her cause but still 'the doorstoppers' flashed their cameras and groundless stories and quotations appeared.

Meanwhile the Prince of Wales was being goaded in India. He is, of course, very experienced in coping with all sorts of questions, particularly where his heart is concerned. One Indian reporter asked his opinion of the Taj Mahal and the Prince replied 'It was a marvellous idea to build something so wonderful . . . to someone one loved so very much.' Indian legend dictates that any bachelor visiting the mausoleum will return with a wife. The obvious question followed and the Prince of Wales stepped neatly around it with 'I might take up the Muslim religion and have lots of wives. That would be much more fun'. At the end of a gruelling but highly successful tour he spent three days trekking in the Himalayas and it was there, free from all official duties, that he could think clearly about Lady Diana and their future together. He returned to London in mid-December fit and rested and went straight down to Windsor to join the rest of his family for Christmas. Lady Diana spent her Christmas at Althorp but returned to London soon after. New Year's Eve was spent in Coleherne Court with a flatmate and the next day she drove to Sandringham, running the gauntlet of the ubiquitous press, to stay for a few days.

Back in London the cat and mouse game continued but Lady Diana had become an expert in foiling her pursuers and met Prince Charles for lunch at Highgrove and again the next day at dawn, at his trainer Nicholas Gaselee's stable in Upper Lambourn in Berkshire where he was 'riding out' his horse, Allibar.

The pressure of the past months had been building up and Lady Diana spent a quiet weekend at Althorp – the 9–11 January 1981 – walking alone

At the end of his official tour of India and Nepal in November 1980, Prince Charles enjoyed three days trekking in the Himalayas.

Prince Charles with his racehorse, Allibar, kept at his trainer Nick Gaselee's stables at Upper Lambourn in Berkshire

about the estate. Two days later she joined the Royal party at Sandringham, for another shoot and left in a borrowed car without being spotted. A thoroughly disgruntled Prince of Wales wished the hoards of pressmen would all go away adding, 'The Queen would be very pleased if you did.'

Once again the Prince of Wales left Lady Diana, this time to go skiing with Charles and Patty Palmer-Tomkinson at their chalet at Klosters in Switzerland. The threat of Europe's pressmen on the slopes robbed Lady Diana of the chance of a skiing holiday. They were reunited a fortnight later, 3 February, at Highgrove.

It was Lady Diana's turn to leave the Prince of Wales, this time for her long-awaited holiday with her mother to their sheep station in Western Australia. The night before she left, she dined with the Prince of Wales in his apartments in Buckingham Palace. It was after dinner that night that he proposed to her. He advised her to think it over carefully while she was away but she accepted him immediately – 'I never had any doubts about it' she confided later.

There was always a bottle of champagne kept in the fridge of Coleherne Court and it was opened, amid scenes of bubbling excitement, the next morning when Lady Diana told her three flatmates of her engagement. That evening, amid the most secret arrangements, Lady Diana boarded a scheduled Qantas 747 with her mother and step-father. Her name was not on the flight list and only the captain knew the identity of his extra passenger. They reached Yass, their sheep station, two days later, completely undetected. The peace and freedom of their Australian home did much for Lady Diana but it was not long, just a day and a half, before the Australian press found her. They descended on the house by road and air and the nightmare had begun all over again.

The press had not bargained for the recourcefulness of Peter Shand Kydd and his wife. They were determined that Lady Diana should have a proper holiday, probably the last such holiday she would ever have. They disappeared to a beach house somewhere in New South Wales. The three of them spent a week relaxing, swimming and body surfing off the near-deserted beach. They discussed the plans for the future, like any mother and newly engaged daughter and caught up on lost sleep. There was still a nagging fear of not knowing when a photographer would discover them or if a reporter would demand an interview. Mrs Shand Kydd decided that her daughter should return to London. The 'escape' was superbly managed and they moved Lady Diana right across Australia and back to her flat without her being recognised.

It was two whole days before Lady Diana was spotted leaving her flat for Highgrove and her fiancé. The thrill of the reunion was clouded the next day. At dawn they arrived at Nicholas Gaselee's stables for the Prince of Wales to 'ride out' Allibar – they were due to race at Chepstow the day after. All went well when he cantered the seven furlongs and as he was walking the horse back towards the stables, the horse shuddered uncontrollably. Lady Diana watched as Prince Charles slipped to the ground but Allibar, his favourite horse, collapsed and died from a heart attack. He was deeply upset and stayed with the horse until the vet certified it to be dead. He carried out his official engagement – receiving the freedom of the City of Swansea on behalf of the Regiment of Wales, while Lady Diana left the stables in the back of an old Land Rover with a coat over her head. It was a terrible day for them both, but it was a sorrow shared.

The secret of the engagement could not be kept for ever. In his chivalrous manner, the Prince of Wales telephoned Earl Spencer at Althorp and asked for his consent to marry his daughter. The consent was readily given. Preparations were made for the announcement and Tuesday, 24 February, was the chosen day. Advance warning was given in coded telegrams to various Ministers of State, Commonwealth Heads of State, ambassadors and other dignitaries including the Archbishop of Canterbury.

On the Monday afternoon, Lady Diana left her flat with Carolyn Pride and dropped her at the underground station at South Kensington. She drove on to St James's Palace to collect her sister, Jane, and then to Buckingham Palace. She parked her red Mini Metro at the end of the 'Visitors Cars Only', in full view of the road. They joined the Queen, Prince Philip, the Prince of Wales – who had just returned from lunching on his former command, the mine hunter HMS *Bronington* – and the Earl and Countess Spencer who were celebrating the news of the engagement.

It was fitting that that night, Lady Diana and her fiancé should be with the two women, their grandmothers, who had done so much for them both. Lady Diana moved into Clarence House with the Queen Mother but went out to dine with her grandmother, Ruth, Lady Fermoy at her flat in Eaton Square. It was a family party with Jane and Robert Fellowes and, of course, the Prince of Wales. A toast was drunk to their future happiness and from then on, Lady Diana Spencer's life would never be the same.

If Kevin Shanley, Lady Diana's hairdresser from Head Lines in South Kensington, had read *The Times* of 24 February or taken notice of the speculation in that morning's edition of *The Sun* he would have known the reason for her 8.30 appointment. She arrived on time, wearing jeans, with her sister Jane. After an hour of his expert care, they returned to Clarence House to change, then to wait at Buckingham Palace, rather nervously, for the official announcement.

That morning, a bright and sunny Tuesday, the Mall was alive with tourists for the Changing of the Guard and there was more activity inside Buckingham Palace, for the Queen was holding an investiture. Nearly 150 men and women assembled in the red and gilt State Ballroom, waiting to receive their awards announced

Lady Diana leaving Coleherne Court with her flatmate Carolyn Pride on her way to Buckingham Palace on the eve of the engagement

in the last New Year's Honours List. They rose as the band of the Coldstream Guards played the National Anthem when the Queen arrived flanked by her courtiers and Yeomen of the Guard. She stood in the centre of the dais and said 'Please be seated'. When the company had sat down on their gilt chairs, the Lord Chamberlain, the former Chief Scout Lord Maclean, came forward and proclaimed 'The Queen has asked me to let you know that an announcement is being made at this moment in the following terms'. Then, reading from the official Court Circular, he continued '*It is with the greatest pleasure that the Queen and the Duke of Edinburgh announce the betrothal of their beloved son, The Prince of Wales, to The Lady Diana Spencer, daughter of the Earl Spencer and the Honourable Mrs Shand Kydd*'. The Queen was smiling broadly and the applause was warm, heartfelt and sustained. Their mood was echoed throughout the nation,

Kevin Shanley, Lady Diana's hairdresser from Head Lines in South Kensington, has cut her hair for many years and still continues to do so.

indeed the whole world as the news flashed out to every continent. The months of waiting and speculation were over.

Lady Diana's first 'ordeal' that day was an interview with the Press Association's Court Correspondent, Grania Forbes. Lady Diana, looking very smart in a deep red velvet suit, red shoes and stockings and a ruffled red and white shirt, was composed but understandably nervous. She sat on the sofa in her fiancé's drawing room and was happy to let him do most of the talking. She was, however only too delighted to show off her engagement ring, chosen by them both from a selection from Garrard and Co, Crown Jewellers. The ring, reputed to have cost £28,500, was a large oval sapphire set with fourteen diamonds on a platinum band.

It was an open interview and both spoke freely. The Prince of Wales, chuckling most of the time, revealed that he was 'positively delighted and frankly amazed that Diana's prepared to take me on'. Lady Diana talked of their meeting when Prince Charles remembered 'this splendid sixteen-year old' and 'what fun she was'. After commenting on the wedding and honeymoon plans and their twelve-year difference in ages, he spoke of her role as the future Princess of Wales. 'I'm sure she will be very, very good . . . she'll be twenty soon, and I was about that age when I started. It's obviously difficult to start with but you just have to take the plunge.' Lady Diana added, 'I'll just take it as it comes' – which, with true foresight, is exactly what she has done.

While they gave another interview to BBC Radio, her father Earl Spencer with Countess Spencer and her son, were outside the Palace. They were spotted by the television crews and Earl Spencer, his voice slightly slurred from the after-effects of his stroke two years before, announced that he was 'very proud, very happy'. He had been taking photographs of the photographers and crowds and they of him. Countess Spencer, in what seemed to be a prepared speech, added 'We're very happy and proud. Very pleased that it is all resolved. I think we both feel enormously proud of Diana, that she's

The Earl and Countess Spencer with her son mingling with the crowds outside Buckingham Palace on the morning of the engagement

taking on such a big responsibility. And she's also a great giver, you know. She's a very generous kind of person. She wants to give rather than take, and that, I think, is most important of all. Don't you?' With that, the Spencer party was swallowed up in the crowd that was growing every minute.

A family lunch followed with the Queen and Prince Andrew who had been given special leave from his helicopter pilot's course at Culdrose in Devon for his twenty-first birthday party at Windsor the Saturday before. He stayed on to be present for the official announcement of the engagement.

After a light lunch, Lady Diana changed into another suit – this time a blue silk number with scalloped edges and a bow belt with a white silk blouse with its light blue swallow motif. At exactly three o'clock the Prince of Wales and Lady Diana arrived, arm-in-arm, on the terrace to the rear of the Palace. Eight carefully selected photographers and cameramen from the BBC and Independent Television were allowed just twelve minutes to record the happy event. They posed on the steps, on that grey and distinctly cold day, then strolled across the lawns below.

Next came the television interview which was conducted inside, in the Bow Room, where it was warmer and brighter. Lady Diana certainly did not show how nervous she was during that fifteen-minute interview

and those in the room commented on how 'natural' she looked. Again she let her more experienced fiancé do most of the talking but when she spoke, she was definite in her answers. The final question was 'And I suppose in love?' With that characteristic gesture of looking out from under the sweep of her hair with those deep blue eyes, a gesture that was to endear her to the nation, she answered softly, but firmly, 'Of course'.

The crowd outside, who had waited patiently for a sight of the engaged couple, were finally rewarded by a glimpse of them as they left Buckingham Palace later that evening. They were driven to Clarence House for a dinner party given by the Queen Mother in their honour. Her devoted friend and courtier, Ruth, Lady Fermoy was also there to make the occasion even happier.

As Lady Diana was staying at Clarence House she appeared briefly on the doorstep after dinner as her fiancé was driven the short distance back to Buckingham Palace. The warm smile and friendly wave to the crowd showed just how happy she was that night.

Engagement

Lady Diana was launched into her new life the second she woke the next day, Wednesday 25 February, in Clarence House. She was also to experience that morning, far too soon for her liking, a part of what was to be a regular feature in their engaged, and later, married life – Prince Charles leaving her for official engagements and tours. She was driven to Buckingham Palace to say goodbye to him by Chief Inspector Paul Officer, one of the Special Branch officers (wrongly

LEFT: *Prince Charles and Lady Diana were reunited in May after a five-week separation at Craigowan on the Balmoral estate where they spent a few days quietly together.*

Prince Charles and Lady Diana photographed together by Lord Snowdon during their engagement

called detectives), attached to the Prince of Wales and recently assigned to Lady Diana with his colleague, Chief Inspector Maclean.

The Prince of Wales left for three days in Scotland and Lady Diana tackled the sackfuls of mail and telegrams of congratulation. She was driven for the last time to Coleherne Court to collect her personal possessions, pausing briefly to say goodbye to the photographers who had practically lived on her doorstep for the last five months. Her mother, Mrs Shand Kydd, arrived from Australia the next

day. Striding through the air terminal with her long legs, reporters had to run to keep up to hear how proud she was of her daugher and thrilled at her engagement. 'I'm sure she can cope and will learn very quickly.' They were united at dinner that night at Robert and Lady Jane Fellowes's apartments at Kensington Palace.

Lady Diana was thrilled to have her mother, her great friend and ally, back in London. She moved out of Clarence House and into her mother's flat in Pimlico. Together they made plans for the wedding like any mother and daughter. They shopped together, quite openly, striding down the pavements, heads slightly bowed. They were rarely recognised as no one

'The Lady Di look' was in and spread even as far as Wellington in New Zealand where these girls were entering in a 'Lady Di' look-alike competition.

expected to see them in the street or in a shop. Lady Diana was sorry to give up her work at her kindergarten just as the children were sorry to see her go. They presented her with an engraved goblet and a selection of their portraits of the future Princess of Wales.

Extra staff were engaged in the Prince of Wales's office at Buckingham Palace to cope with the volume of congratulatory mail. A former assistant private secretary of the Prince of Wales, Oliver Everett, was brought back from the British Embassy in Madrid as a temporary aide for Lady Diana. He is now a permanent member of her household.

As was to be expected, Lady Diana soon became a leader of fashion. 'The Lady Diana look' was *in* and designers copied her clothes. Another mark of her independence and fashion sense was her choice of designers for her wedding dress, David and Elizabeth Emanuel. They had made a blouse she had modelled when Lord Snowdon had photographed her for a Vogue feature and she admired their work. They also made the black taffeta evening dress she wore to her first official engagement, a recital in aid of the Covent Garden Opera House at the Goldsmiths' Hall in London. Although the strapless, low-cut dress caused a stir, it was not dissimilar to the one worn by the Queen, as Princess Elizabeth shortly after her engagement to Prince Philip.

The Prince of Wales had bought a replacement for Allibar, a gelding called Good Prospect and had made sure that the afternoons of Friday 13 March and the following Tuesday were kept free for he was riding at Sandown and Cheltenham. Lady Diana went to both meetings and saw her fiancé unseated both times. His pride was hurt more than his person.

Their engagement was given its final blessing by the Privy Council. Under the terms of the 1772 Act of Succession no British royal descendents of George II can marry without the monarch's approval.

Another separation, this time for five weeks, came when the Prince of Wales left on 29 March for his tour of New Zealand, Australia, Venezuela and America. It was a sad parting for them both on that rain-swept runway at Heathrow and there were tears in her eyes as she watched the RAF VC10 take off. They were, however, able to speak to each other every day by telephone.

Every day, some detail of the arrangements for the wedding was issued by Buckingham Palace. St Paul's Cathedral was chosen in preference to Westminster Abbey as it held more people and the route from the Palace was longer. Coincidentally, St Paul's stands on the Roman site of the Temple to Diana, the goddess of hunting and virginity. An edict from the Lord Chamberlain was issued for the makers of wedding memorabilia. Lord Snowdon headed a team to decide what was 'tasteful' and what was not. T-shirts bearing portraits of Lady Diana, the Prince of Wales or the Royal Arms were definitely out. There were thousands of souvenirs, not all made in Britain, that flooded on to the market. In a fever of patriotism, every conceivable, and inconceivable article bore their portraits or arms – cheap mugs and ashtrays, commemorative plates and glasses right up to expensive jewellery,

Friday 13 March proved to be an unlucky day for Prince Charles and his new racehorse, Good Prospect, when he fell at the eighteenth fence during a steeplechase at Sandown Park. Fortunately, both horse and rider were unhurt.

gold and silver ornaments. It was a welcome boost to the potteries, hard hit by the recession and many jobs were temporarily saved by the sudden demand. Stamps and coins throughout the Commonwealth were issued with their portraits and at the Chelsea Flower Show there was intense rivalry among the growers for their rose to be chosen to be called 'The Lady Diana'.

There was much for Lady Diana to do during those weeks her fiancé was away. She visited dressmakers and designers, milliners and shoemakers – adding to her wardrobe and putting her trousseau together.

Shortly before the Prince of Wales left Australia, a report appeared in a West German magazine that they had bought the transcript of a telephone conversation between him and Lady Diana and were going to publish the 'scoop'. The tapes turned out to be a forgery and the injunction taken out by the Prince's solicitors preventing their publication in Britain was, in the end, unnecessary.

Another storm, this time electrical, hit the scheduled British Airways flight from Heathrow to Aberdeen that flew Lady Diana to join the Prince of Wales at Balmoral on Sunday 3 May but she arrived safely that evening. Balmoral Castle is far too large to open up for a couple for a few days, so the Royal Family use another smaller house on the estate, Craigowan. They stayed there for six days, relaxing or salmon fishing on the River Dee.

Back in London the official visits began again. Lady Diana's name began to appear regularly in the Court Circular columns, planting a tree at Broadlands when the Mountbatten Exhibition was opened, present at the lunch at Windsor Castle given for the President of Ghana or watching the Queen present the new Colours to the 1st Battalion, Welsh Guards.

A country girl at heart, Lady Diana naturally prefers country engagements. It was particularly enjoyable for her to attend a service of dedication at St Mary's, the parish church of Tetbury, the local town of Highgrove – her future home. They were cheered by the enthusiastic townsfolk as they walked to the new operating theatre the Prince of Wales opened later.

During the State visit of King Khaled of Saudia Arabia Lady Diana attended a banquet at Buckingham

ABOVE: *Wedgwood souvenirs produced in honour of Prince Charles's wedding*
BELOW: *Lady Diana being enthusiastically received on her first visit to Tetbury*

Palace in his honour and another given by him at Claridges Hotel. The more of these functions she attended, the more her confidence built up. Gradually she became used to the crowds that were cheering her, the countless eyes that were focused solely on her. With her easy charm she captivated everyone she met – from visiting Royalty to an estate worker, from a Head of State to any one of the crowds who thronged to see her. Even at Royal Ascot, the Mecca of fine horse racing and fashion, Lady Diana stole the show driving down the course in the Royal procession in her latest creation. Another ball, another dress – this time for a ball given for 600 people to celebrate Prince Andrew's twenty-first and Prince Philip's sixtieth birthdays.

Her engagements were varied in the 'run up' to the wedding – one night to the première of *For Your Eyes Only*, the latest James Bond Film where she sat next to the star, Roger Moore, another at a soirée at the Royal Academy of Arts in Piccadilly or a Military Musical Pageant at Wembley Stadium where the Prince of Wales took the salute. Again Lady Diana was in her element at a garden party

BELOW: *Lady Diana looking stunning in a red dress at the première of the latest James Bond film,* For Your Eyes Only. *During the film, Lady Diana sat next to the actor, Roger Moore who played the part of James Bond.*

ABOVE: *Lady Diana at Nicholas Soames's wedding where Prince Charles was best man*
BELOW: *Lady Diana attended Royal Ascot wearing a striking new outfit each day*

ABOVE: *Lady Diana leaving St Paul's with Prince Charles and Prince Andrew after a wedding rehearsal*
RIGHT: *A few days before the wedding, Lady Diana watched Prince Charles play polo for England II against Spain at Smith's Lawn, Windsor Great Park. She is wearing the gold watch and bracelet which were a recent birthday present from Prince Charles and also his watch whilst he was playing polo.*

given for the tenantry of the Duchy of Cornwall on the lawns of Highgrove on 30 June – the day before her twentieth birthday. This she celebrated at Buckingham Palace with a small party of family and friends – a far cry from the quiet supper she had with her flatmate, Virginia Pitman, on her nineteenth birthday.

Lady Diana, like all her Fermoy relations, is a keen tennis player and avid supporter of the Wimbledon fortnight. She watched most of the games on television and spent three afternoons in the Royal Box where she saw both the men's and ladies' finals with one or other of her sisters.

The countdown to the wedding was on. There were the final fittings for the dress at Emanuels and the rehearsals at St Paul's Cathedral. The strain was also mounting. At a

polo match at Tidworth in Hampshire the cameramen and photographers did not let up their constant surveillance of Lady Diana for a second. She left in tears, escorted by Lady Romsey and was driven back to Broadlands by her Special Branch police officer. All was well again the next day, Sunday 26 July, when she watched her fiancé play polo for England II against Spain from the safety of the Royal Enclosure. The Prince of Wales's team won 10–5.

On Monday night, two days before the wedding, the Queen gave a ball at Buckingham Palace with a dinner party for the close friends of the Royal Family before. It was a magnificent affair and in a way served as a wedding reception, as only a few selected guests were to come to the wedding breakfast. By this time Lady Diana

had moved back into Clarence House.

The night before the wedding, Lady Diana and the Queen Mother spent the evening quietly watching the television coverage of the spectacular firework display in Hyde Park in London. Well over half a million people flooded into the park to witness the Prince of Wales light the first of one hundred and one beacons and, with the Queen and most members of the Royal Family and the distinguished foreign wedding guests, watched a recreation of the fireworks originally staged to Handel's 'Music for the Royal Fireworks'.

When Lady Diana went to bed that night she was a commoner. In the morning, she was to marry the man she loved before the eyes of the whole world and begin her life as a member of the Royal Family.

CHAPTER FIVE

Wedding Day

It is not difficult to see why the Royal Wedding, which in reality affected the lives of but two people, was the most unforgettable and glorious day in royal history. Its origins were an illusory fairy tale. Add to that, the traditions of a thousand years of monarchy, the British love of pageantry and their ability to stage manage such an event, and you come close to the reason why that remarkable day was watched by 750 million television viewers and arrested the world throughout seventy nations.

On 29 July 1981 the eyes of that

LEFT: *The Prince and Princess of Wales photographed by Lord Lichfield in the Throne Room at Buckingham Palace*

The Prince and Princess of Wales, returning to Buckingham Palace, received a tumultuous reception from the crowds.

world were focused on the route between Buckingham Palace and St Paul's Cathedral, on such London landmarks as the Mall, with its red tarmacaddam surface, Trafalgar Square, the Strand, Fleet Street, the home of the national newspapers, and Ludgate Hill, the entrance to the City of London. Two miles of street and pavement, of squares and crescents, hotels, offices and houses on that day, were overflowing with people. Many had been there all night, some for days but most arrived at dawn. It was a

beautiful day and the warmth and jollity of the crowd was infectious – they cheered anything that moved, the dust cart, the police vans and the horses.

It was an early start at Clarence House that morning. Lady Diana was soon joined by her mother, step-father, Peter Shand Kydd, and brother, Viscount Althorp. The Queen Mother, however, stayed in bed until the last moment as she had only recently recovered from a leg infection. There was a certain nervousness in the air, as would be natural in any household before a family wedding and, despite the pomp and glamour, the reportage and its magnitude, that is exactly what it was

Lady Diana on her way to St Paul's in the Glass Coach with her father, Earl Spencer. This was to be her last journey as a commoner.

– a family wedding. Mrs Shand Kydd, with a ladies' maid Evelyn, helped Lady Diana to dress. Her hairdresser had arrived early and when his part was done she was made up by the beautician, Barbara Daly. The wedding dress, the most closely guarded secret, was a triumph for its designers, David and Elizabeth Emanuel. It was an apt creation with its blend of the theatrical and the romantic. Made of ivory pure silk taffeta with an over-layer of pearl-encrusted lace, the dress had a bodice with a low frilled neckline and full sleeves gathered at the elbow. In keeping with tradition, the bride wore something old – the Carrickmacross lace that made up the panels had once belonged to Queen Mary and had now been dyed a slightly lighter shade of ivory than the dress; something new – the dress itself; something borrowed – her mother's diamond earrings and the Spencer tiara and something blue – a tiny blue bow had been stitched into the waist band. The sweeping train was twenty-five feet long and trimmed with sparkling lace and the veil was hand-embroidered with tiny mother-of-pearl sequins and pearls. Hardly noticeable in those overflow-

ing folds of taffeta was a minute gold horseshoe studded with diamonds, for luck. Almost hidden under the full petticoats, the bride's slippers were no less ornate. The silk shoes had a central heart motif made of nearly 150 pearls and 500 sequins.

It was an early start, too, for the two pages and five bridesmaids who arrived, the younger ones with their parents, through a back entrance to change and leave from Clarence House. The pages were Lord Nicholas Windsor, the eleven-year-old son of the Duke and Duchess of Kent and Edward van Cutsem, the eight-year-old son of the Prince of Wales's friend, Hugh van Cutsem. The brides-maids were also chosen as daughters of friends or family. The chief brides-maid was Lady Sarah Armstrong-Jones, daughter of Princess Margaret and the Earl of Snowdon. She is a 'veteran' bridesmaid having attended, among others, her cousin, Princess Anne in 1973 and the Princess of Wales's sister, Lady Sarah Spencer at

her wedding in 1980. She was assisted by Miss India Hicks, Earl Mount-batten's granddaughter and youngest daughter of David and Lady Pamela Hicks. Next came Sarah Jane Gaselee, the ten-year-old daughter of the Prince's racehorse trainer. Then the two youngest, Clementine Hambro, just five years old and great-grand-daughter of Sir Winston Churchill and her namesake, his wife Clemen-tine. She had been one of the bride's charges at her kindergarten school. She teamed up with Catherine Cameron, the daughter of other close friends of the Prince of Wales, Donald and Lady Cecil Cameron of Locheil, daughter of the Marquess of Lothian. While the pages wore the 1863 Royal Navy cadet's summer uniform, the bridesmaids were dressed by the Emanuels in the same vogue as the bride. Lady Sarah's dress was a longer version of the Victorian style brides-maid's dresses, with their flounced and scalloped calf-length frocks and their garlands and baskets of summer flowers. Their sashes and shoes matched the yellow of the 'Mount-batten rose', a poignant reminder of 'The Honourary Grandfather' who was missing from the guest list. The

The bridesmaids entering St Paul's

same golden Mountbatten roses were in the bouquet, along with white fresias, lily of the valley, stephanotis, white Odontoglossum orchids and trailing ivy leaves. A nice Royal touch, the leaves of myrtle and veronica from bushes planted from Queen Victoria's bouquet still growing at her home Osborne, in the Isle of Wight, were woven into the creation.

Earl Spencer arrived at Clarence House shortly before the Queen Mother left for Buckingham Palace by car to join the Queen's Carriage Procession.

Meanwhile, the 2,600 guests had been arriving at St Paul's Cathedral since 9.30. Apart from members of Europe's Royal Family and those from Africa and the Middle East, the Heads of State (including Nancy Reagan, the wife of the United States President, Ronald Reagan) and the leaders of the Commonwealth, the politicians, the civil servants and the diplomats, there were members of the Queen's staff from all her residences and some of the tenantry from the Duchy of Cornwall. There were also Spencer and Fermoy friends and relations from Norfolk, Scotland and

Northamptonshire. Lady Diana's closest childhood and school friends, her school mistresses – sadly her favourite 'Ally', Miss Gertrude Allen, died shortly before the wedding – were also there to see their popular and prized pupil married. In the front row on the bride's side were her three flatmates, in prime position to give her moral support.

The Glass Coach left Buckingham Palace for Clarence House at 10.20, just as Mrs Shand Kydd, her husband and son left the bride and drove by car the two miles to the Cathedral. Through the open front door, the bride could hear the waves of cheering as they left, followed shortly after by her pages and bridesmaids in another two cars. She could hear the tremendous roar from the crowd when the Queen's Carriage Procession, led by two squadrons of the Sovereign's Escort, appeared through the centre arch of Buckingham Palace. The Queen was in the first of eight Semi-State Postillion landaus with the Duke of Edinburgh. A light rug covered the Queen's lap, despite the warm summer sunshine. She wore a

fine-pleated turquoise coat and dress with a floral hat, while the Duke of Edinburgh, in deference to the bridegroom's Service, wore the uniform of Admiral of the Fleet. When the second carriage appeared there was a particularly excited cheer when the crowd recognised the Queen Mother, so becoming in her seagreen silk georgette and hat of matching flowers and osprey feathers, and her grandson, Prince Edward. The third carriage brought Princess Margaret and Anne, Captain Mark Phillips and Viscount Linley followed by the Gloucesters in the fourth carriage, the Duke and Duchess, his mother the Dowager Duchess and his five-year-old son, the Earl of Ulster. The fifth, sixth and seventh carriages took the Duke of Kent and all of his family, his brother Prince Michael and his family followed by their sister, Princess Alexandra and all the Ogilvys. The last carriage brought the senior members of the Queen's Household.

Following very quickly afterwards, came the Carriage Procession of the Prince of Wales with his Sovereign's Escort. The bridegroom travelled with his brother, Prince Andrew who was his chief 'supporter' – the best man in royal parlance (the other supporter was his brother Prince Edward). They both wore Royal Navy uniform, the Bridegroom, in his full ceremonial dress uniform of a commander with a blue Garter sash; his brother, a midshipman, in his No 1's. To those who know Prince Charles well, they would have noticed a certain tight grimace on his face which denotes tension as he waved to the enthusiastic crowd, an understandable tension as one of the footmen behind was a Special Branch police offier in disguise.

At precisely 10.37, the moment that everyone had been waiting for, the Glass Coach left Clarence House. Drawn by two of the Windsor Greys, Lady Penelope and St David, and driven by a senior coachman, Richard Boland, they clattered out into the Mall to a tumultuous welcome. Despite the wide glass windows, the crowd and television cameras could only catch a glimpse of the bride with her veil right down over her face, and her father, Earl Spencer. Flanked by an escort of the Mounted Police for her last journey as a commoner, she arrived at the West Door of St Paul's Cathedral

twenty minutes later. The footmen jumped to the ground, one opening the door of the coach. Lady Sarah Armstrong-Jones and India Hicks arranged the Bride's train, white on the deep red carpet. She took her father's arm, he in turn being supported by an aide, and mounted the steps to a fanfare of trumpets.

Just inside the door, the bride was welcomed by the Archbishop of Canterbury, Dr Robert Runcie, the Dean of St Paul's, the Very Reverend Alan Webster, and the Bishop of London, the Right Reverend Graham Leonard. There was a short delay as David and Elizabeth Emanuel arranged the wedding dress, veil and train, then the bride's procession formed up.

The cathedral clock struck eleven. On the first chime the organist, Sir David Wilcocks, with the orchestra began 'The Trumpet Voluntary' (The Prince of Denmark's March) by Jeremiah Clarke. The Bride's procession was led by the verger, followed by the Archbishop's chaplain bearing the Primatial Cross, then the Arch-

The bridal procession setting out on the three-and-a-half minute walk up the aisle

RIGHT: *Prince Charles turns round to greet Lady Diana as she arrives with her father at the dais under the Great Dome where the marriage ceremony was to take place.*

bishop of Canterbury himself. Behind him came the Bishop, the Dean, the Archdeacon and the Precentor – a veritable array of rich copes and tall, pointed mitres. There were worries that Earl Spencer might not be up to the great ordeal and his son, Viscount Althorp, was standing by. He was not needed and the proud father took the bride on his arm up to the steps of the high altar. The procession took three-and-a-half minutes to walk up the nave, the bride smiling every inch of the way. The bridegroom, with his two supporters, the Princes Andrew and Edward had moved to the dais. He turned to see his bride, unable to bear the suspense any longer and smiled encouragingly. Just like any parish church wedding, the bridegroom's family sat on the right of the cathedral, the Queen, the Duke of Edinburgh and the Queen Mother sat beside the dais, with Princess Margaret and Viscount Linley and Princess Anne and Captain Mark Phillips

A view of the bride and groom's families and other guests during the marriage service

sitting behind. On the bride's side, on the left of the dais sat her mother, her brother Charles and grandmother, Ruth, Lady Fermoy, with her sisters, Sarah and Jane and their husbands behind.

The music and hymns had been chosen with great care by them both and Prince Charles had said 'I want everyone to come out having had a marvellous, musical and emotional experience.' They had also chosen an amalgam of the Church of England Series One marriage service and some prayers from the New Alternative Service Book.

The Dean of St Paul's opened the service and then the Archbishop of Canterbury took over for the solemnisation of matrimony. His clear sonorous voice was relayed by loudspeaker to the crowds outside, further down the route they listened on transistor radios and after each response a loud cheer went up. The bride answered in a strong, clear voice although rather high pitched. The bridegroom smiled at her and she, through her nervousness managed to smile back at him. Their hands were clasped throughout the ceremony and every so often he gave a reassuring

squeeze. His responses were firm and dignified.

The bride had decided to omit the words 'to obey' from her vows, a depearature from all other royal weddings. She made, however, a slight mistake with the bridegroom's many Christian names, reversing the order of the first two. He in turn left out a word from his vows and declared 'all *thy* goods I thee endow' as he placed the ring on her finger. The ring was made with the last of a gold nugget found in Wales sixty years ago – the rest had been used for the Queen Mother in 1923, the Queen 1947, Princess Margaret 1960 and Princess Anne in 1973.

The Archbishop blessed the bride and bridegroom and prayed that they would 'ever remain in perfect love and peace together'. He joined their right hands together and pronounced them man and wife – the Prince and Princess of Wales. At that moment the loudest cheer of all went up throughout the crowds, in front of television sets and radios the world over. Earl

Spencer was led back to a seat beside Mrs Shand Kydd by his son as the rest of the congregation were seated. The choirs of St Paul's Cathedral and Her Majesty's Chapel Royal sang 'O let the nations rejoice and be glad', a new anthem written for the occasion by the Welsh composer, William Mathias. In that true ecumenical service, the Speaker of the House of Commons, Mr George Thomas, an ardent Methodist, read the lesson from Chapter 13 from the First Book of Corinthians.

The Archbishop then gave his address. His opening echoed the thoughts of all those who heard him – 'Here is the stuff of which fairy tales are made: the Prince and Princess on their wedding day.' He continued in the same vein 'But fairy tales usually end at this point with the simple phrase: "They lived happily ever after". This may be because fairy stories regard marriage as an anticlimax after the romance of the courtship.' He expanded on their role in life and their responsibilities of 'creating a more loving world'.

While the bride and bridegroom moved up to the high altar, the choirs sang another anthem, Charles

Parry's Psalm 122. After the prayers, which were led by a former Archbishop of Canterbury, Lord Coggan, and followed by the Roman Catholic Cardinal of Westminster, Basil Hume, more prayers were said by the Moderator of the Church of Scotland, the Right Reverend Andrew Doig. The short prayers said by these august prelates were out of all proportion to the significance of their presence in that Church of England ceremony. The Reverend Harry Williams, former Dean of the Prince of Wales's Cambridge college, Trinity, read the last prayer.

The sumptuous wedding ended with a hymn chosen by the bride, 'I vow to thee my country', with those apt words to the rousing music of Gustav Holst. The final blessing was given by the Archbishop of Canterbury to the kneeling congregation, who then stood for the National Anthem sung to the new arrangement by Sir David Wilcocks. The Archbishop then preceded the bride and bridegroom to the south aisle for the signing of the register. She signed 'Diana Spencer' for the last time; he signed just 'Charles P'. The other witnesses were the Queen, Prince Philip, the Queen Mother, Prince Andrew and Prince Edward, Princess Anne and Lady Sarah Armstrong-Jones and the bride's family signatures included her parents, Earl Spencer and the Hon Mrs Shand Kydd and her grandmother, Ruth, Lady Fermoy. By the register, they could hear the haunting notes of the Maori opera soprano, Kiri Te Kanawa, with the Bach choir as they sang the aria 'Let the bright seraphim' by Handel.

When the witnesses had returned to their seats, the State Trumpeters, high up in the Whispering Gallery, sounded off a fanfare that filled the cathedral. When the bride, the Princess of Wales re-appeared with her husband, she had her veil back from her face. Still with their hands firmly clasped, fingers entwined, they advanced to the dais. They began their procession appropriately with the strains of Elgar's 'Pomp and Circumstance March No 4 in G'. When they drew level with the Queen, the Princess of Wales dropped to a low curtsy; he bowed to his mother, she smiled across at hers. As they moved down the aisle, their attendants, beautifully 'managed' by Lady Sarah Armstrong-Jones, followed behind. Just like any other family wedding, the bridegroom's mother came down the aisle with the bride's father and the bride's mother with the Duke of Edinburgh. As the Prince and Princess of Wales paused at the top of the West Door a peal of twelve bells from the northwest tower started the bells in every other church in the City of London, as well as the seventeen-ton Great Paul bell in the southwest tower of the Cathedral. The Princess waved to the ecstatic crowd before descending to the 1902 State Postillion landau that was to take them back to Buckingham Palace for the wedding breakfast.

The cheering, unceasing all the way, was an open display of the love and loyalty the people had for their new Prince and Princess of Wales. Behind them, in the Queen Alexandra's State Coach, came Prince Edward and three of the bridesmaids while they in turn were followed by the Glass Coach bringing the other attendants. The Queen followed with Earl Spencer; the Duke of Edinburgh and Mrs Shand Kydd came next, closely followed by the Queen Mother, drawing as always a special cheer from the crowd. The last five carriages brought 'the cousins' back.

The carriages moved off at a brisk pace and the procession quickly clattered into the quadrangle of the Palace to the applause of the Household staff. Once all the carriages had passed down the Mall, the police slowly advanced in line before the crowd, allowing them to fill up every inch of space in front of the Palace railings. Upstairs in the Centre Room of the Palace, two liveried footmen opened the french windows on to the balcony to the cries of 'We want Charlie', 'We want Di'. The Prince and Princess of Wales came out to a tumultuous welcome, which was long, heartfelt and sustained. They were joined by the whole wedding party. In all, there were five balcony appearances. At the instigation of Prince Andrew, the crowd were rewarded on the fourth appearance

The Prince and Princess of Wales arrive back at Buckingham Palace

ABOVE: *The Prince and Princess of Wales photographed with their families*
LEFT: *An informal photograph of the happy bride and groom relaxing with their attendants after the more formal photographs had been taken*

with the Prince of Wales kissing his beautiful bride.

The wedding photographs were taken by Patrick Lichfield, a cousin of the Queen, in the Throne Room and afterwards the guests went down to the Ball Supper Room for the wedding breakfast. There, the 118 close friends and family sat down to a three-course luncheon of brill with a lobster sauce, a dish the Palace chefs named *suprême de volaille Princesse de Galles*, and strawberries and cream, each course served with a different wine. The Prince and Princess of Wales cut the enormous wedding cake with his dress sword and he replied on behalf of them both to a toast for their future happiness jointly proposed by the Princes Andrew and Edward.

At 4.20, the State Postillion Landau appeared through the central arch of Buckingham Palace. Another fun touch, to show that it was a family wedding and not a state occasion, was

ABOVE: *Prince Charles leans over his bride who has sat down to rest on the steps of the throne*
LEFT: *The newly weds wave to the crowds as they cross Westminster Bridge on their way to Waterloo Station at the start of the honeymoon*

the helium-filled balloons emblazoned with Prince of Wales's Feathers and the sign, 'Just Married' with hearts, written in lipstick on a piece of old cardboard on the back of the landau that took them to Waterloo Station. Again they were cheered all the way to Waterloo Station, the full crowd waiting for a glimpse of the Princess of Wales's 'going away' outfit. They were not disappointed for she looked stunning in a coral pink dress of canteloupe silk with that characteristic white organza frilled neckline, worn with a matching bolero. She wore a hat with a jaunty turned-up brim decorated with ostrich feathers and around her throat was a five-strand pearl choker.

The landau drove straight onto the platform and stopped beside their train, three carriages drawn by an engine which was appropriately named *Broadlands*.

CHAPTER SIX

Honeymoon

It was essential for the Prince and Princess of Wales to have as long together as quietly as possible as man and wife, before the strains of position, responsibility and public engagements were added to the novelty of their married life.

They began their honeymoon, like that of his parents thirty-four years before, at Broadlands in Hampshire, the former home of Lord Mountbatten, and now lent to the couple by the Prince's cousin and friend, Lord Romsey.

The train arrived at Romsey station from Waterloo shortly after 6 o'clock. As the Prince and Princess of Wales stepped on to the platform, they looked happy and relaxed, despite

The happy Prince and Princess of Wales enjoyed watching Britannia's *departure from Gibraltar.*

the rigours of the day. The cheers of the jubilant crowd rang out with the peals of bells from Romsey Abbey as the car drove them the half mile to the house. The huge, black Palmerston gate clanged shut and, for the first time for months, their time belonged to no one but themselves. For the three days of their visit to Broadlands, the Prince and Princess of Wales slept in the Portico and Green rooms with their fabulous view over the sweeping lawns and river beyond.

The 6,000 acre estate was virtually under seige by the Hampshire police

keeping the press and other well-wishers at bay. The couple spent their time just walking around the estate, swimming in the heated outdoor pool and in the early evenings, Prince Charles fished alone on the 400-yard stretch of the River Test that flows within the walled grounds. His lack of success on the river or the rain did little to dampen their spirits. On the Saturday morning, 1 August, they were driven in the rain to Eastleigh Airport where they boarded an Andover of the Queen's Flight for Gibraltar to join the Royal Yacht *Britannia*. That morning, and indeed every moment of her life to come when she is 'on view', the Princess's clothes were of special interest. For

RIGHT: *Broadlands near Romsey, Hampshire; formerly the home of the famous British Prime Minister, Lord Palmerston, and of Earl Mountbatten, it now belongs to Lord Romsey, Earl Mountbatten's grandson and cousin of Prince Charles.*
BELOW: *The Prince and Princess of Wales leaving Eastleigh Airport on 1 August on their way to join the Royal Yacht Britannia in Gibraltar*

the journey she wore a white-spotted silk skirt with bright blue and red flowers, a tie top and a cornflower blouse.

The decision to leave from Gibraltar caused a diplomatic storm and the King and Queen of Spain, having initially accepted their invitation to the wedding, announced that they could not attend and stayed at home in Spain.

During part of the four-hour flight, the Prince piloted the aircraft himself. Upon arrival at Gibraltar, they were driven through flag-bedecked streets in an open-topped Triumph Stag car, rather too fast for the patriotic Gibraltarians, to the Naval Dockyard. They boarded the Royal Yacht to the peals of every church bell in the colony and to the strains of Rod Stewart's song, 'Sailing' played by the military band on the quayside. All around the harbour, ships' sirens hooted, yachts and light craft milled about the bay – even the fire-fighting tugs let off volley after volley from their water cannon.

Once the official farewells had been said to the Governor and local dignitaries, their honeymoon proper began. The Princess was overcome by their reception, pausing just once to brush aside a tear of happiness. They stood, hand-in-hand by the stern rails and waved goodbye. As the Royal Yacht left Gibraltar and steamed into the Mediterranean Sea and out of sight it seemed like a fairy-tale end to a fairy-tale story.

The arrangements for the honeymoon had been left to the Prince's private secretary, the Honourable Edward Adeane. His brief was to take them where they could insure privacy, away from the press. His plans were the most closely guarded secret and the lack of reports in the newspapers on the honeymoon was a testament to his success. Reports that H.M. Yacht *Britannia* was heading for Malta or Sardinia or the island of Capri off Naples sent the inhabitants into a

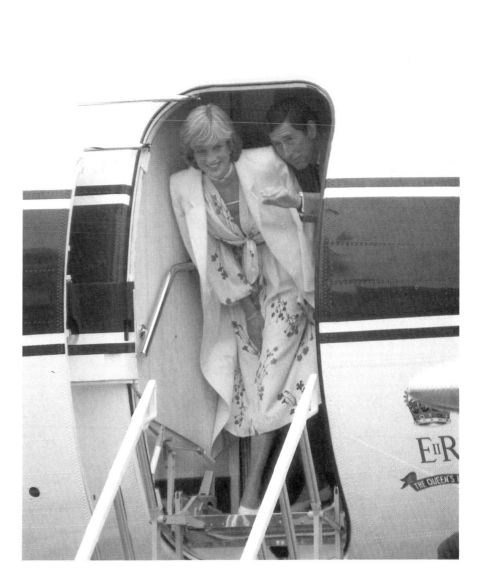

ABOVE: *The Royal Yacht* Britannia *was surrounded by a flotilla of small craft as it steamed out of Gibraltar.*
BELOW: *The Princess of Wales looking suntanned in a pair of white Bermuda shorts when the Royal Yacht* Britannia *reached Port Said in Egypt*

flurry of excitement but the rumours turned out to be false. Instead the Royal honeymooners enjoyed the first part of their cruise at sea, landing nowhere. They occupied the royal bedroom on the upper deck and used the state rooms below. It was a time to relax. They swam in the swimming pool, sunbathed on the afterdeck. They lunched and dined with the members of their Household and some of the officers and after dinner the whole party watched a recording of their wedding or one of the feature films that were on board.

The first positive sighting of the elusive Royal Yacht was their meeting with an Italian warship on 7 August – a full week after they left Gibraltar. The destroyer, the *Sagittario*, passed in the morning with the crews of both vessels lining the sides. They raised their caps and shouted their 'Hurra' to the Royal couple as

Britannia steamed into the Ionian Sea.

She was making for the tiny 'Homeric' island of Ithaka, the home of Odysseus, off the west coast of Greece, just below the holiday island of Corfu. Their visit took the islanders by surprise, but not the military who had been alerted to keep prying helicopters out of the area. The Royal Yacht anchored overnight in Skinos Bay, about a mile from the island's capital, Vathi. The Prince and Princess were able to slip ashore to a secluded bay that afternoon where he swam in the warm, clear water while his wife lay on the beach in her deep red, one-piece bathing suit. In the morning they went ashore with their party, visiting a Greek shipping magnate at his villa. They were thoroughly relaxed and in fine spirits but word came that the press were arriving in droves and it was decided to shelve the tour of the island. *Britannia* headed out to sea shortly before lunch on the Saturday accompanied by a Greek gun boat. It was a nice touch to include this romantic little island in their itinerary as it was there that Penelope, the faithful wife of Odysseus, waited twenty-one years for his return from the Trojan Wars.

The Royal Yacht steamed on in total privacy. A press aide at Buckingham Palace remarked 'All honeymooners are entitled to be left alone. I would think that everyone in the country is absolutely delighted they haven't been seen.' They were seen, rather glimpsed, as they passed the Island of Rhodes on their way to Port Said in Egypt.

There, as everywhere, the crowds were out in force to greet the Royal couple. They were fit, very tanned and ecstatically happy. That night, 12 August, President Sadat and his wife, Jihan dined on board the Royal Yacht. After dinner the Prince received one of Egypt's highest honours, the Order of the Republic First Class. It was a short visit and *Britannia* continued down the narrow Suez Canal and the Gulf of Suez to the mouth of the Red Sea. This time she made for the tiny islands off the resort town of Hurghada, famous for its coral reefs. There, they swam in the warm sea and the Prince went scuba diving.

On the morning of 15 August, President Sadat and his wife flew down to say farewell to the Prince and Princess of Wales. As they boarded the steps of their RAF VC10

The Prince and Princess of Wales arriving at R.A.F. Lossiemouth in Scotland on their way to join the rest of the Royal Family at Balmoral

the Princess turned and blew a kiss to their hosts. Their aeroplane landed at R.A.F. Lossiemouth in Morayshire and, after a brief talk with some of the crowd that came to welcome them back, they were driven to Balmoral to join the Queen and the rest of the members of the Royal Family on their summer holiday. Prince Charles was to return to Egypt all too soon – to attend the funeral of the President assassinated on 6 October 1981.

CHAPTER SEVEN

Balmoral Holiday

Traditionally Balmoral is the most fun of all the royal residences and the Princess of Wales happily joined the relaxed routine of the Castle for the second part of her honeymoon. She knew the 'form' and enjoyed the life and the traditions of the place, like the Queen's Pipe Major playing the bagpipes outside the window at breakfast or the picnics in the croft 'up the fell'.

Balmoral is also a sporting estate

LEFT: *The Prince and Princess of Wales looking tanned and relaxed as they posed for photographers by the banks of the River Dee a few days after returning from their Mediterranean honeymoon cruise*

Balmoral Castle is set in the heart of the Highlands of Scotland.

and she knew that she would lose her new husband to the grouse moor, the salmon river and the stalking moor, although not for ever as there were always the shooting lunches and the drives where she was allowed to squeeze into his butt with his loader. He taught her the finer points of fly-fishing, just as the Queen Mother had taught him on the same stretch of the River Dee at Birkhall. Their efforts went unrewarded as the river was too low for the salmon to come upstream.

The Royal Family worship at the little Craithie church not a quarter of a mile from the gates of Balmoral.

That first Sunday, 16 August, the crowds had gathered early to see the Royal Family, in particular, the latest member. They were rewarded with a glimpse of the Princess in her white suit, ruffled polka dot blouse and a summery wide-brimmed hat. The Right Reverend Andrew Doig, the Moderator of the Church of Scotland who said one of the prayers at their wedding, gave the address on the subject of 'Bring forth fruit'.

It was a very confident Princess that met the press the following Wednesday. In the hope of seeing the press off the estate, the couple had agreed to be photographed. The Prince chose a romantic setting, the historic Bridge of Dee by the Ballochbuie Forest and

The still suntanned Princess of Wales, wearing a wide-brimmed straw hat, on her way to Craithie Church one Sunday morning whilst continuing her honeymoon with the Prince of Wales at Balmoral

they obligingly walked hand-in-hand towards them. As the cameras clicked, they joked with the throng. The Princess described her honeymoon as 'fabulous' and on married life 'I can highly recommend it'. The Prince, with typical goonish humour said 'A very happy Christmas to you all' – a direct reference to the fracas at Sandringham just after the New Year when they met on less happy terms. Her smile vanished when asked if she had cooked breakfast for her husband yet; 'I don't eat breakfast' she replied in a voice that warned off any more too familiar questions. She faced the cameras, her head held high and laughed most of the time. She teased the cameramen asking if the bouquet they had given her had been put down on expenses. Both sides left, highly delighted at the interview. Two days later, 21 August, a special family party was given at Balmoral for Princess Margaret's fifty-first birthday.

Royal wedding fever was still as much alive in London as at Balmoral. Just one week after the wedding on 5 August, the hottest day for two years, a selection of the 6,000 wedding presents went on view in the Throne and Entrée Rooms at St James's Palace. On that first day, three thousand people queued for up to six hours to see the 1,200 presents, the wedding dress, veil, train and the wedding slippers. On display were not only the exotic presents from heads of state – jewellery, pictures,

glass, porcelain, rugs and carpets but also practical items like vacuum cleaners and food mixers. There were also many charming presents, like the ubiquitous portraits of the Royal Family drawn by children from all over Great Britain. The presents from the members of the Royal Family, like the dining table made by Lord Linley at his specialist furniture and woodworking school, were not on view. Over 207,000 people saw the

exhibition and the money raised from the exhibition, around £85,000, went to charities connected with the disabled and sick children. The wedding dress, a bridesmaid's dress and a page boy's uniform, together with a different selection of about 200 presents are being shown all over the country. The exhibition closed in London on 4 October and opened in Cardiff Castle on 10 December. The next move was to Edinburgh on 2 February where the presents went on display at the Palace of Holyrood House.

Another 'crowd puller' was the portrait of the Princess of Wales by Bryan Organ in the National Portrait Gallery. It was an informal picture of the Princess wearing trousers in front of a door, with no handle, in Buckingham Palace. On 29 August, a student slashed the painting in three places and ripped the canvas from top to bottom. The magistrate did not believe his plea that it was a political act for Northern Ireland and fined him £1,000 and sent him to prison for six months. The picture is now restored and on view behind perspex.

On 2 September the Princess paid a flying visit to London to see the wedding presents and dashed down to Highgrove to meet her interior decorator. She used the scheduled flight from Aberdeen and travelled as Mrs Smith, the name of her Special Branch officer who accompanied her.

A selection from the vast array of wedding presents on display in St James's Palace. The glass bowl in the centre of the table was given by the President of the United States and Mrs Reagan.

The slippers worn by the Princess of Wales on her wedding day. Made by Clive Shilton of Covent Garden, London, the exquisite shoes, covered in ivory silk, had a heart-shaped decoration on the front personally selected by the bride.

The Braemar Gathering attracted more people than ever before on Saturday 5 September. The Princess was again the centre of attention, the games and Highland dancing being secondary. There were a few tense and anxious moments but she carried the day with her usual dazzling smile. At one point, she and Prince Charles received an icy glance from the Queen when she continued to talk and giggle, inadvertently, after the start of the National Anthem.

Balmoral was closed up when the Queen's party and her staff returned to London on 21 September. The Prince and Princess of Wales were to enjoy another month in Scotland, staying at Craigowan. They were both gloriously happy in their new house and the Princess had more time to explore the area. It was also a time to spend with her husband, away from his family, to *really* get to know him and, of course, he to know his twenty-year-old bride.

In London, Buckingham Palace announced that three ladies-in-waiting had been appointed to the Princess of Wales. Miss Anne Beckwith-Smith, a former West Heath pupil, is full time while the Honourable Lavinia Baring and Mrs James West are unpaid but they all share the duties.

The Young England Kindergarten had a pleasant surprise when the Princess paid another visit to London and Highgrove on 14 October. She took the opportunity while the Prince of Wales went south to tour the riot-stricken areas of Toxteth and Birmingham. Again travelling as Mrs Smith with her Special Branch officer she took the flight to Heathrow. Driving herself, she made an unscheduled visit to the kindergarten to roars of excitement from her former charges. At Highgrove she made the final arrangements for the furniture that was arriving from London the next day, then she went back to London and the flight to Aberdeen.

Honeymoons, whoever you are, do not last for ever. For the hardworking Prince of Wales there were already calls upon his time and person and in his absence, a heavy programme had been arranged for the next three months. Within that busy schedule, the Princess of Wales had been given a few official functions, supposedly minor, to 'break her in gently'. With great foresight and judgement, the aides agreed upon their first engagement – a three-day tour of Wales. Despite their great confidence in her, they could not have foreseen the 'Princess of Wales fever' that was to sweep the Principality.

The Princess of Wales attended the Braemar Gathering on 5 September with other members of the Royal Family. For the Highland occasion, the Princess aptly wore a striking plaid suit and black tam o'shanter.

CHAPTER EIGHT

Tour of Wales

The Welsh are renowned as a musical nation, high in emotion and rich in love. For the visit of the Prince and Princess of Wales they displayed all three traits towards their Princess in such abundance and with such fervour that it surprised the most ardent royalists. Not even the driving rain and bitter cold could dampen their enthusiasm for a single minute of that three-day tour in November which took them over four hundred miles throughout the Principality.

For the first time since the Prince of Wales entered the public eye he was

LEFT: *For the first day of the tour, the Princess of Wales wore the national Welsh colours of red and green*

Prince Charles presenting the new Princess of Wales to the Welsh people from Queen Eleanor's Gate in Caernarfon Castle

not the centre of attention. Naturally, the Welsh wanted to see their Prince but it was his wife whom they really wanted to meet and, when they did, they were not disappointed. From the moment she stepped off the royal train at the industrial town of Shotton in the north to the end of the tour in Cardiff the Welsh suffered a severe bout of 'Princess of Wales fever'. They loved her for her charm and naturalness, her youth and her beauty and her deliberate choice of clothes – like her first outfit of poppy-red jacket

worn with a green pleated skirt and red wide-brimmed straw hat, the national colours of Wales.

The first day was the turn of north Wales. The Princess was nervous at the daunting task ahead of her but at the first strains of Ceirwen Stuart's harp at the Deeside leisure centre at Queensferry she began to relax and to enjoy herself. The Prince had met the harpist before when she had played for him before his Investitute in 1969. At their first walkabout in the seaside resort of Rhyl the Princess, shepherded by her lady-in-waiting, Anne Beckwith-Smith (also on her first tour of duty), launched out to meet the large crowd. She was an instant success. She shook the

The Princess of Wales at Caernarfon Castle seated on the slate podium, the site of Prince Charles's investiture in 1969 as Prince of Wales

a royal tour after Welsh extremists had threatened to disrupt the royal visit. An incendiary device was found by the police at an Army recruiting office at Pontypridd. A letter had been delivered to the BBC studios in Bangor from a small extremist group calling themselves *Meibion Glyndwr* – the 'Sons of Snowdonia'. It said 'We will not forget 1969 – beware Caernarfon', presumably a reference to the Investiture when two of their members were blown up by their own bomb.

The crowds at Caernarfon knew nothing of the threat and the Prince and Princess of Wales showed no hint of concern when they arrived at the castle. The only incident of the whole tour happened here when a woman broke out of the crowd and sprayed the royal Rolls-Royce with paint. The Earl of Snowdon, Constable of Caernarfon Castle, conducted Prince Charles and his wife into the grounds of the thirteenth-century castle and introduced members of the staff. Afterwards, they talked to Scouts and Guides, drum majorettes and the children's choir. Then they moved to the slate podium and sat on the stools at the exact spot where the Queen had invested the Prince of Wales. Some children sang a song, rather prettily in Welsh about Noah's Ark. After that, Lord Snowdon escorted them to the Queen's Gate. It was an historic moment, full of symbolism when the Prince presented the Princess of Wales to the people. The crowd below chanted 'God Bless the Princess of Wales'.

The second day was the turn of central and west Wales to receive their Prince and Princess. Security, already tight, was stepped up when an incendiary bomb was found at the British Steel Corporation headquarters at Cardiff.

Their first engagement was to attend the bilingual service to mark the 800th anniversary of St David's Cathedral. Despite the atrocious weather conditions, the Prince and Princess of Wales insisted they carried out all their planned walkabouts. That day she was marginally warmer in a beige cashmere coat, a beige tweed suit and a cream shirt and a small brimmed hat in camel velvet with ostrich feathers and veil. Once again, she captivated the crowds, shaking hands, a few words at each stop, then moving on to the next group. That day, the many gifts of

hundreds of outstretched hands, knelt down to talk to countless numbers of children, giving each a special smile and just the right words. Her brand of chat endeared her to everyone whom she met. One woman, who had been waiting hours in the cold was rewarded by the Princess saying 'Poor you – I feel cold myself – my hands are freezing and you must be much worse. Thank you for waiting for us.' Later the woman confided, 'She's so sympathetic to us – you can sense it.' And her words summed up the feelings of the whole Principality. They felt that she was talking *with* them rather than *at* them, despite all the bustle around her. Bouquets and small presents were showered on them both, thanked for and then passed

down the line of aides to the escorting police.

They moved on to Llandudno where the Prince of Wales opened a new conference centre. He apologised for being late – 'Wales is a surprisingly large place when you try to drive around it.' The real reason was the enthusiasm of his wife in talking to the people.

At Bangor there was the first hint of protest when militant students chanted 'Go home English Princess' and 'Go home Charlie'. The Princess merely ignored the shouts and stink bombs and deliberately went to talk to the children immediately below the protesters until steered away by her husband. It was one of the tightest security operations ever mounted on

ABOVE: *Despite the torrential rain at Carmarthen on the second day, the Princess of Wales chatted enthusiastically to the crowds lining the route*
RIGHT: *The Princess wore a beige cashmere coat with a matching hat trimmed with ostrich feathers and an eye-veil.*

flowers were received with her first words of Welsh – *Diolch* – 'thank you'. The Prince took second place in their attention as they pleaded 'Diana love, over here'. One old man in St David's broke down and cried with happiness, pulled himself together, only to break down and cry again.

The Prince and Princess of Wales took the train to Carmarthen where they lunched at the agricultural college. Later they left for Llandeil where they had tea. It was typical of the Princess to lower her umbrella to afford the crowd, some of whom had been waiting for five hours in the pouring rain, a better view. Through these extended walkabouts they were late leaving for their final engagement of that day, a gala concert in Swansea. That was a happy evening and the Princess, wearing an emerald green taffeta dress with an emerald and

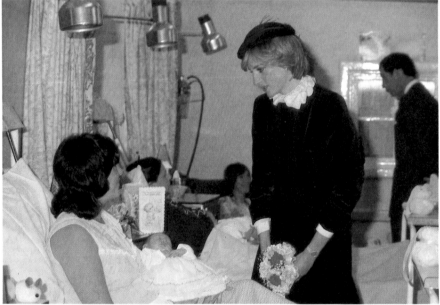

TOP LEFT: *For the gala concert at Swansea, the Princess of Wales wore a striking emerald taffeta dress with an emerald and diamond necklace and earrings*
TOP RIGHT: *On the third and final day of the tour, the Princess of Wales wore a deep burgundy-coloured velvet suit with a matching bowler-style hat. Standing beside her is her full-time lady-in-waiting, Miss Anne Beckwith-Smith.*
ABOVE: *The Princess of Wales talking to a mother and her new-born baby in the maternity ward of Llwynypia*

diamond choker and earrings, chatted with some of the three-hundred young musicians.

The last day of the tour was to the middle and south of Wales ending up the capital, Cardiff. The day started with bright sunshine and the Prince and Princess of Wales visited the town of Builth Wells and the Royal Welsh Showground. There they received some more substantial presents – a black Welsh heifer, a black Welsh mountain sheep and two armchairs. They were sent on to Highgrove as a happy memory of their tour. The Princess wore a burgundy velvet suit with black trimmings about the cuffs, a ruffled cream silk shirt with a matching bowler-style hat trimmed with an ostrich feather.

The weather did not hold and the rain fell hard and fast. The crowd turned out to cheer in their thousands. At Brecon, one lucky little boy was given a small bar of chocolate by the Princess, even a baby was kissed by her. They drove on to Llwynypia to the hospital for lunch. After lunch there was a slight change of plan and the Prince of Wales accompanied his wife to the maternity ward. There he talked to a mother who had had a baby daughter during the night and gave the first indication of his approaching fatherhood. He thought that it was a very good thing for fathers to be present at the birth of their children and added to the attendant pressmen, 'I expect I'll get a lot of letters about that'.

Outside the hospital, in the driving rain, the Ferndale Male Voice Choir sang 'God Bless the Prince of Wales' as they left for Pontypridd, the gateway to the Rhondda Valley. There, work stopped, factories and shops closed, shifts at the mines ended early as the loyal inhabitants lined the streets and cheered until they were all hoarse. The Prince and Princess went on to Newport before going to Cardiff for the grand finale of the triumphant tour.

At the City Hall that night, the Princess of Wales was granted the freedom of the City of Cardiff. To the intense delight of all present, she included in her first public speech of thanks a few words of Welsh. She swore an oath of allegiance to the Lord Mayor and promised to 'Obey his Warrants, Precepts and Commands'.

As they drove away from the City Hall the tour of Wales was over. It had been a unqualified success for everybody. The Princess of Wales had put everything she had into making it a success and had shown that she was ready, and able, to perform her duties to the full. The Welsh in return, had loved her for it. The Prince of Wales was undeniably proud of his young wife. They worked well together as a team, he keeping a watchful eye on her, keeping her as far as possible on schedule.

RIGHT: *The Princess of Wales leaving Cardiff City Hall where she had made her first speech in Welsh at the end of her triumphant tour of Wales*

CHAPTER NINE

Homes and Palaces

The Princess of Wales has the use of many houses throughout Great Britain, from the Scilly Isles to the north of Scotland but there are only two that she thinks of as home. Her main residence is Highgrove House, near Tetbury in Gloucestershire, while their official London residence is within Kensington Palace.

Highgrove is an ideal house for the Prince and Princess of Wales to start their married life. It is set in one of the prettiest parts of England, the South Cotswolds in the hamlet of Doughton. Princess Anne found it for her brother who had been looking for some time for a house in that area. Built of the local Cotswold stone at the end of the eighteenth century, it is

Highgrove House in the hamlet of Doughton near Tetbury was bought by Prince Charles in 1980.

a compact Georgian house with its four reception rooms, nine bedrooms (some with a dressing room and bathroom attached), all the usual 'kitchen offices' and staff rooms as well as the now 'essential' nursery wing.

In the summer of 1980, the Conservative MP, Maurice Macmillan wanted to move closer to his ageing father, the former Prime Minister, Harold Macmillan who lives in Sussex. He put up Highgrove House and its surrounding 348 acres for auction but it was bought prior to sale by private treaty by the Prince of

Wales for an undisclosed sum. It is in an ideal position being not far from Windsor and London, nor from the Duchy of Cornwall and the Prince's estates. He can hunt with the Beaufort Hunt and play polo at Cirencester. Although the Princess does not care for horses, she does enjoy living in the country. They have many friends in the area as well as family – Princess Anne and Captain Mark Phillips live eight miles away at Gatcombe Park with their two children, Peter aged four and Zara born in May 1981, and Prince and Princess Michael of Kent live at Nether Lypiatt with their two children, Lord Frederick Windsor, two-and-a-half years old, and his sister, Lady Gabriela, born in

RIGHT: *The townspeople of Tetbury raised money for presenting the Prince and Princess of Wales with new gates for Highgrove as a wedding present. Hector Cole, a local wrought iron craftsman, was commissioned to make the gates to a design chosen by the Prince and Princess of Wales. Working in his forge, Mr Cole spent five hundred hours making the gates.*
BELOW: *The old gates of Highgrove*

April 1981. Undoubtedly, these cousins will become boon companions for the Princess of Wales's children, being born and living so close together in time and place.

The Prince of Wales began redecorating Highgrove before his engagement with the help of a neighbour, Mrs Andrew Parker-Bowles. On a practical note, the downstairs windows have bulletproof glass as the house can clearly be seen from the road. The South African-born interior decorator, Dudley Poplak, was brought in to co-ordinate his ideas with the wishes of the Prince of Wales and his fiancée Lady Diana. After a race against time to complete the alterations and decorations before the Prince and Princess of Wales came back from Balmoral, the house is now finished. The workmen, all local,

BELOW: *The Prince of Wales pub in a quiet backwater of Tetbury with the landlords, Colin and Susan Dyer. The name was chosen in 1880, long before the Prince of Wales bought Highgrove.*

The South Front of Kensington Palace, the London home of the Prince and Princess of Wales

moved out and the removal men arrived with their furniture, some of it wedding presents chosen by the Princess of Wales, some pieces either given or lent from other Royal Houses and the rest personal pieces that they had both cherished in their bachelor days.

Highgrove House is very much 'home' to the Prince and Princess of Wales. It is there that they live in very much the same style as their other landed neighbours. They have a housekeeper who manages the house and does a little cooking and a full-time gardener. They have been joined by a cook, Miss Rosanna Lloyd, who was chosen after months of careful searching. The army gave the Prince and Princess of Wales a swimming pool as a wedding present which has to be installed.

The Prince and Princess of Wales's London apartments, uninspiringly just called '8 and 9', are in the north-west corner of Kensington Palace but appropriately they look out on the Prince of Wales's arcaded courtyard one side and a walled garden on the other. That part of the palace was added by King George I in the 1720s and the first incumbent was his ugly mistress, the Duchess of Kendal.

From then on, the apartments were used for members of the Royal Family or as grace and favour houses for loyal members of their Household. The Countess Granville lived in Number 8 for nearly fifty years, moving out just before World War II – her husband, Earl Granville, was lord-in-waiting to Queen Victoria, Kings Edward VII and George V. During the war, that part of the palace was badly damaged by fire-bomb attacks. Fortunately, the fine Georgian staircase and much of the ornate William Kent plasterwork was undamaged but later the rot set in and the fabric of the rooms deteriorated.

Restoration work started in the northwest corner in 1975 and has taken six years to complete. Where possible, the fine plasterwork has been restored and the staircase, the main feature of the apartment, has been renovated to its former glory. The layout on the first floor has also been adapted to give the Prince and Princess a large drawing room, over-looking the courtyard, a library-study for him and a sitting room for her and a dining room. On the second floor they have their master bedroom with its dressing rooms and bathroom and two additional bedrooms. The nursery wing is also on that floor. The kitchens, offices and staff quarters are on the ground floor.

The Princess will have many friends in that rabbit warren of a palace when they move in during the summer, not least her sister Jane in the Old Barracks just behind the palace, Princess Margaret and her children in another wing with various Gloucester and Kent cousins close by.

CHAPTER TEN

Married Life

The positive adulation of the Princess of Wales was not confined to that Principality. Now firmly established in her home, Highgrove, she had a base from which to carry out her official duties. On Sunday night, 2 November, she was invited to a concert at Blenheim Palace and afterwards she dined with the Duke, her distant cousin, and the Duchess of Marlborough. The next evening the crowds gathered in London for a glimpse of her as she attended the opening of the 25th London Film Festival at the National Film Theatre.

The following day, the Princess attended her first grand ceremony – the State Opening of Parliament. She travelled to the Houses of Parliament

The Princess of Wales travelling in the Glass Coach to the State Opening of Parliament. This was the first state occasion that she had attended since her wedding three months earlier.

with Prince Charles, Princess Anne and her husband, Captain Mark Phillips, in the Glass Coach, the same carriage that had carried her to St Paul's for her wedding just three months before. She walked in the procession with her husband just behind the Queen and Prince Philip and took her seat below them and to the right. As the Queen delivered her Speech from the Throne in the House of Lords, she sat composed and serene, exchanging the occasional smile with

Prince Charles. That evening it was difficult to judge who outshone whom at the opening of the exhibition 'The Splendours of the Gonzaga' at the Victoria and Albert Museum. The Princess had chosen a magnificent white silk décolleté evening dress with a blue sash and bows worn with her pearl choker and matching bracelet. Afterwards she and the Prince of Wales were due to dine with the Italian Ambassador but she felt unwell and the dinner was cancelled. The real reason was revealed the next day.

Eleven o'clock in the morning seems to be the hour that Buckingham Palace makes its important announcements and at that hour on 5 November the Press Secretary put out a

bulletin to say that the Princess of Wales was expecting a baby in June 1982. The bulletin continued 'The Prince and Princess of Wales, the Queen and the Duke of Edinburgh and members of both families are delighted by the news. The Queen was informed personally by the Prince and Princess.

LEFT: *The Princess of Wales at the opening of the exhibition, 'The Splendours of the Gonzaga' at the Victoria and Albert Museum. Looking like a fairytale princess, she wore a dazzling hand-painted silk dress.*

The Prince and Princess of Wales listening to the Queen reading her speech during the State Opening of Parliament. The Princess of Wales is wearing the tiara given to her as a wedding present by the Queen.

'The Princess is in excellent health and her doctor during the pregnancy will be Mr George Pinker, Surgeon Gynaecologist to the Queen.

'The Princess hopes to continue to undertake some public engagements but regrets any disappointment which may be caused by any curtailment of her planned programme.

'The baby will be second in line to the throne.'

The announcement was a contrast to the one made by the Palace in 1948 which simply read 'Her Royal Highness, the Princess Elizabeth, Duchess of Edinburgh, will undertake no public engagements after the end of June' and left everyone to draw their own conclusions. Another departure from royal form was to make the pregnancy known so early but that was in order to stop the advance preparations for the proposed royal tour of New Zealand, Australia and Canada in the New Year.

Prince Charles replying to the Lord Mayor's speech with the Princess of Wales looking on.

That day, the Prince and Princess of Wales attended a lunch in their honour given by the Lord Mayor of London, Sir Robert Gardner-Thorpe. Six hundred guests filled the magnificent Guildhall and applauded them loudly. The Prince made only a passing reference to his good news but the Lord Mayor, in his hastily re-written speech, spoke in romantic and flowery terms – 'The magic of the Royal Wedding has provided a memory that glows with the ever-lasting lustre of a gold ingot, a gold ingot that has now been supremely hallmarked by this morning's announcement that Your Royal Highnesses are to be blessed with a child, which we all rejoice remembering that babies are bits of stardust blown from the hand of God.' Guests, like the crowds outside on the route back to Buckingham Palace, cheered loudly. There seemed to be a new chapter to the 'fairy-tale princess' every day.

Seemingly quite undaunted by her pregnancy, the Princess of Wales attended the Festival of Remembrance at the Albert Hall on the Saturday evening. The next day, Sunday 9 November, she joined the Queen Mother, King Olav of Norway and others on the balcony

LEFT: *The Princess of Wales leaving the Guildhall after she and Prince Charles had attended a lunch given in their honour by the Lord Mayor of London*

overlooking the Cenotaph. There she watched the Queen lead the nation in mouring for the dead of two World Wars. The morning proved too much for her and she cancelled her appointment in the afternoon.

The tenantry of the Duchy of Cornwall were naturally disappointed when their Duchess cancelled her visit but they quite understood. Prince Charles explained her absence, 'You have all got wives – you know the problems. She is all right, but it is better not to do too many things.'

Buckingham Palace then added 'The Princess has made it known that she will try to make as many public appearances as possible, but if she does not feel well she will have to withdraw. In her condition she is bound to have some days off.'

Feeling distinctly unwell, the Princess of Wales put a brave face on the problems of early pregnancy when she visited the National Railway Museum in York. She was rather quiet and subdued as they toured the museum together and as she watched Prince Charles ride on a miniature railway. Later in the day she opened a new shopping centre in Chesterfield in Derbyshire and hundreds of people handed her gifts for her baby. Two extra police cars were summoned to take away the thousand posies and the toys. They were a sympathetic crowd and the Princess admitted that 'No one told me that I would feel like I did' – almost the same words that Prince Charles used after his first parachute jump.

The Prince of Wales's birthday, 14 November, was spent at Sandringham and the couple stayed there for the week-end. It was a very different scene on that Friday to the year before when rumours were rife that he would announce his engagement.

Still feeling unwell, the Princess cancelled her trip to Bristol on Monday 17 November and stayed behind at Highgrove while Prince Charles went alone.

The Princess of Wales watching the Remembrance Day Service at the Cenotaph with Queen Elizabeth the Queen Mother, King Olav of Norway and Princess Alice, Duchess of Gloucester

ABOVE: *The Princess of Wales, wearing a black Spanish-type sombrero hat and cape, talking to a group of well-wishers at Chesterfield a few days after the announcement of her pregnancy*
BELOW: *During her walkabout in Chesterfield, the Princess was given so many bouquets of flowers that two extra police cars were called to take them away.*

Up to then, all her major engagements had been carried out with the Prince of Wales. Her first solo engagement came the next evening when she switched on the Christmas lights in Regent Street. The event was televised live and seen by millions of viewers. She met the singer, Cilla Black and when she forgot to introduce her husband, the Princess ribbed her saying, 'You mustn't forget your better half', adding that she had left hers behind watching 'the telly'. She told the organisers that she was '. . . fine, I'm feeling much better'. For that occasion, she wore a midnight-blue velvet suit with silver piping round the collar, a peach silk blouse with silver shoes.

In a touching ceremony the Prince and Princess planted five trees in Hyde Park in London on 19 November. They planted a tulip tree together in honour of their impending baby. She then planted a mountain ash to commemorate their wedding and Prince Charles in turn planted three cherry trees in memory of his uncle, Earl Mountbatten. Afterwards, they had lunch at the Royal Thames Yacht Club in Knightsbridge where the Prince is Commodore.

Her next solo public engagement gave the Princess particular pleasure when she opened the new Post Office administrative centre in Northampton as it afforded her the chance to return, for the first time since her wedding, to Althorp. She arrived by helicopter and landed on the gravel drive outside the house. Now being Royal, her father, Earl Spencer, gave a neck bow to his daughter and the Countess curtsied. Although they had met fairly regularly in London, they had much to catch up on over lunch. They had not much time, however, and she was soon off to Northampton where she was cheered by an enthusiastic crowd of 10,000.

The first house party at Highgrove was given over the weekend of 4–7 December. It was mostly a family affair with the Princess's sister, Lady Sarah McCorquodale and her husband Neil, Lady Sarah Armstrong-Jones, Prince Charles's old friend, Nicholas Soames and his wife, Caroline, and also a polo-playing friend, Lord Patrick Beresford. As the

RIGHT: *The Princess of Wales at the tree-planting ceremony in Hyde Park on 19 November*

ABOVE: *One of the Princess of Wales's first solo engagements was to open the new Post Office administrative centre in Northampton.*

RIGHT: *The Prince and Princess of Wales attending a concert of music at Tetbury parish church shortly before Christmas*

Princess danced with her husband outside their front door the long lenses of the press, standing on the road, picked up the whole party.

On Tuesday 8 December the editors of Fleet Street were invited to Buckingham Palace by the Queen. Through her press secretary, Michael Shea, she made an appeal for the newsmen to let up on their constant and unbending surveillance of the Princess of Wales. It was a plea not from the Monarch but from a mother who was concerned for her daughter-in-law. The Princess, in her third month of pregnancy, was beginning to show signs of stress. Her independance and freedom were threatened, not by any official or Royal directives but by the photographers camped at her gate. Her every move in the grounds of her home was recorded, the quick dash into Tetbury for some

ABOVE: *The Princess of Wales paid an informal visit to the local school in Tetbury shortly before Christmas where she joined in singing carols. An ardent fan of The Muppet Show, the Princess's Kermit the Frog mascot can be seen on the bonnet of her Ford Escort.*
RIGHT: *The Princess of Wales leaving the Royal Opera House, Covent Garden after attending a Christmas party*

trivial item was captured and appeared on the front pages the next day. The editors responded and agreed to cover only official engagements and call off their newshounds.

Despite the attentions of these photographers and the announcement that the Princess of Wales would cut down on her official functions, she still managed to attend a few local engagements. On 9 December she braved the snow to visit the St Mary's Junior School in her local town of Tetbury. Four days later, dressed in Cossack-style coat trimmed with fur, she and the Prince of Wales drove to a service in Gloucester Cathedral.

The Queen is reported as saying 'Our family comes in all sizes these

The Prince and Princess of Wales outside St George's Chapel, Windsor, after matins on Christmas Day

days – there is always plenty of variety'. By tradition, the Royal Family come together for Christmas at Windsor Castle. They all met on Christmas Eve, and on Christmas Day the whole family attended matins at St George's Chapel. Again, in keeping with tradition, the party breaks

LEFT: *The Princess of Wales, wearing a striking blue coat with appliqué designs, visiting a school in Tulse Hill, London*

up and various members of the family meet again at Sandringham for the New Year. It was a very different scene from the year before as, mindful of the Queen's wish for privacy, the hordes of photographers stayed away. The Princess of Wales was back in the place of her childhood. She revelled

in the familiarity of Sandringham and caught up with memories of her old haunts and the news of friends.

At heart, the Princess of Wales is very much a country girl but, for the short time that she has been exposed to the public life, she has shown a sophistication and strength, coupled with an ever-increasing beauty, that has gained her the respect and love of the nation and admiration of the whole world.

CHAPTER ELEVEN

Princesses of Wales

When Prince Charles married The Lady Diana Spencer on 29 July 1981, it was the first marriage of a Prince of Wales that was not an arranged match for over six hundred years.

In 1361, Edward of Woodstock, better known as the Black Prince, married his cousin and childhood companion, Joan, the Fair Maid of Kent. It was undoubtedly a love match between that 'valiant and gentle Prince of Wales, the flower of chivalry in all the world at that time' and '*la plus belle de tout d'Angleterre*' – the most beautiful woman in England. He was thirty-one and heir to the English throne and Aquitaine in France, a decided 'catch' for any foreign power. Joan, Countess of Kent in her own right, was two years older than him and a widow of doubtful reputation. She had bigamously married the Earl of Salisbury at the age of sixteen when her true husband was serving his King in France. Her wedding to

A sixteenth-century Flemish tapestry showing the betrothal of Prince Arthur and Catherine of Aragon

the Prince of Wales was a sumptuous affair and their life together, mostly spent in France, was rich and eventful.

The next Princess of Wales, Lady Anne Neville, was a tragic pawn in her father's manipulation of the Wars of the Roses. This daughter of 'Warwick the Kingmaker', was betrothed in 1470 at Angers in northern France to Edward of Westminster, the fifth Prince of Wales and son of the unstable Henry VI and the redoubtable Margaret of Anjou. The 'beauteous, right virtuous, and full gracious' Lady Anne was just sixteen and he, 'a well-featured young man' was just a year older. Their life together was short lived for that 'gallant springing young Plantagenet' was killed eight months later at the Battle of Tewkesbury. She then

married Richard of Gloucester and became his queen when he ascended the throne as Richard III.

The marriage of the next Princess of Wales, Catherine of Aragon to the sickly son of Henry VII, Prince Arthur, was as luckless as her predecessor, lasting only five months. The couple had been engaged practically since birth to cement the alliance between England and Spain. They were married in 1501 in the old St Paul's Cathedral with magnificent celebrations afterwards. The King, anxious to appease the Welsh, sent their prince and princess to live at Ludlow Castle where he died of the plague shortly afterwards. Eight years later, the Princess of Wales married her brother-in-law, who by then was King Henry VIII.

The three Hanovarian Princesses of Wales in the eighteenth century had little in common apart from an intense hatred of their husbands'

family, a hatred that was reciprocated. The first, Caroline of Anspach, was a clever and beautiful woman with a genuine appreciation of the arts. She married in 1705, George Augustus of Hanover, the eldest son and heir of the future George I. The Hanovarians came to England in 1714 and immediately set up rival political establishments, the Princess of Wales supporting the Whigs against the King's Tories. He branded her 'that she-devil' after she criticised his protégé, the Tory Robert Walpole. At one point, relations between father and son were so bad that the King ordered his arrest. It was no secret that the Princess of Wales was the dominant partner of the marriage, and on his succession as King George II, in 1727, it was Queen Caroline who manipulated the Government.

The friction between the Princess of Wales and the King was nothing compared with her pathological hatred of her eldest son, Frederick Louis. Frederick, known after his death as 'Poor Fred', had been kept in Hanover until he was twenty-one. It was he, the fifteenth Prince of Wales, who nearly married the Lady Diana Spencer for her dowry of £100,000. He eventually married the Princess Augusta of Saxe-Gotha in 1736 when she was seventeen. She was never to become queen, for her husband predeceased his father. Her influence on the monarchy was to come later, for this formidable and possessive woman bullied her eldest son with commands of 'George, be King' after his accession as George III.

LEFT: *Lady Anne Neville, the second Princess of Wales, is seen here in the elaborate court clothes of the fourteenth century*
BELOW: *Augusta, Princess of Wales, wearing a black veil to indicate her recent widowhood, seated with her children beneath a portrait of her late husband. Painted by George Knapton in 1751 soon after the death of Frederick, Prince of Wales.*

LEFT: *A formal painting of Princess Alexandra who was Princess of Wales for nearly forty years. Painted by Sir Luke Fildes in 1893 a few years before Princess Alexandra became Queen.*

The wife of the seventeenth Prince of Wales, Princess Caroline of Brunswick, was an unmitigating disaster. When, in April 1795, he first saw the stocky little woman of twenty-six, talkative and foolish, the Prince declared to his aide, 'Harris, I am not well, pray get me a brandy'.

The conception of their daughter, Princess Charlotte, on their wedding night was probably the only consummation of their marriage. A separation followed and she left the country on an extended tour with an assortment of lovers. On the Prince Regent's accession in 1820, 'Prinny' tried, unsuccessfully, to divorce her. She died soon after and neither came out of the shameful affair with much credit.

The last of the Hanoverians, Queen Victoria, personally vetted the girl her 'darling Albert' had chosen to marry their son, Albert Edward, the eighteenth Prince of Wales. She was Princess Alexandra, daughter of the 'grandfather of Europe', Prince Christian IX of Denmark. The nation – and the Prince of Wales – immediately fell for this beautiful girl of eighteen with her great strength of character and charm. She was to be Princess of Wales for nearly forty years, Queen for only nine and Queen Mother for the last fifteen years of her life.

The penultimate Princess of Wales was also chosen by Queen Victoria.

Queen Mary in 1911, soon after she became Queen. A great-granddaughter of George III, she lived until 1955.

Caroline of Brunswick was married very unsuccessfully to the Prince Regent in 1795. Painted by Sir Thomas Lawrence in 1804.

She believed that her wayward eldest grandson, the Duke of Clarence, needed 'a good sensible wife with some considerable character'. The candidate was Princess May of Teck, a great-granddaughter of George III. Before the wedding took place, Prince 'Eddy' died of pneumonia and this 'very nice girl, *distinguée* looking, with a pretty figure' married his younger brother, Prince George, later created Prince of Wales on the accession of his father, Edward VII. She was a tireless worker and a great support to her husband when he in turn succeeded as George V in 1910. The august and revered Queen Mary, the grandmother of the Queen, survived her husband for another eighteen years.

Our Princess of Wales is only the ninth to bear that noble title in nearly seven hundred years, as opposed to the twenty-one Princes of Wales. Behind her lies a tradition of service to King and Country. Before her, God willing, she can look forward to many years as Princess of Wales (rumours that the Queen will abdicate in favour of her son are totally unfounded). It may take some time for her to 'learn the ropes' but she has already shown that she will be an *active* Princess of Wales and when the time comes for her to become Queen Consort, she will be well prepared for her role.

OVERLEAF: *The first official portrait of the ninth Princess of Wales painted when she was still Lady Diana Spencer. Painted by Bryan Organ in 1981.*